TESTS
FOR THE
OUTPUT-ORIENTED
MANAGER

T E S T S

FOR THE

OUTPUT
ORIENTED
MANAGER

A Self-Assessment Guide

BILL REDDIN Ph.D.

KOGAN
PAGE

DEDICATION

This book is dedicated to Florence Snodgrass, my first instructor in psychology. I think she taught me more than she knew. Fact.

Kogan Page Limited
120 Pentonville Road
London N1 9JN

© W. J. Reddin, 1991.

British Library Cataloguing in Publication Data

A CIP catalogue record for this book is available from the British Library.

ISBN 0-7494-0250-4

Typeset by CG Graphic Services, Aylesbury, Bucks
Printed and bound in Great Britain by
Richard Clay Ltd, The Chaucer Press, Bungay, Suffolk

Contents

Part IV: Further Application

Preface

The absolutely central aim of this book is to improve the self-awareness of managers so that they will be able to become more effective.

The process towards becoming more effective must start with self-awareness, then move to situational awareness and then to either changing the situation or changing one's behaviour in a situation. Using behaviour appropriate to the situation is the route to becoming more effective. There can be no other logic.

There is one person in this world we all want to know better – ourself. This book can help you along that voyage. The wise words of Socrates, Confucius and Lao Tzu that echo in our ears have all proposed 'Know thyself', and obviously we all know ourselves to a degree. The aim of this book is to increase that degree.

Certainly, the book starts by focusing closely on one's own self – that is partly what self-awareness is about. But then there is an action component, and in its final chapters this book helps you with that. You start with self-awareness and then engage the action component.

We also need to go back to Burns –

> *Oh wad some pow'r the giftie gie us*
> *To see ousels as ithers see us!*
> *It wad frae monie a blunder free us,*
> *An' foolish notion.*

Readers with knowledge of my earlier work may be surprised that I have written a book on what is, essentially, personality. My previous writing fell into some very clear categories. I started with work on managerial style, following with managerial situations and then, finally, managerial effectiveness. I took what might be considered to be a behavioural approach to most of these issues. As I worked with both large and small clients on style, situation and effectiveness it became clearer to me that the issue of personality is central in organizations and must be squarely addressed.

All my books on management up to now have been concerned with a fierce emphasis on 'Outputs'. I defined an output as 'the extent to which a manager achieves the outputs of the position'. I have been very much concerned with behaviour but, until this book, I have not really 'gone inside a manager's head'. This book does. It aims to help those who want to become more output-oriented to think not only of their job design and its measurement, together with the behaviour that is most appropriate, but also to help them in looking at their own more effective or less effective behaviour and to think about how to improve it.

This book can be used in several ways, as Chapter 2 illustrates. You can complete your tests all at one sitting and just for yourself. You can complete the tests one by one and discuss each one with others. Use it in the way which is most comfortable for you. The book is quite definitely good for a plane trip!

As a manager you well know that sometimes you cause the problem, sometimes others cause the problem, or sometimes the situation is a problem in itself. This book cannot solve the problems but it will increase your self-insight to better identify the source of the problem so as to more effectively do something about it.

Some things you should change, some things you should not change, some things you should use far more than you do now. It depends on how accurate your perception is of yourself and how accurate your perception is of your situation. This book cannot go further than that.

So, what should be your ideal style? Sorry, this book

will not answer that. Situations are different, workplaces are different, the moment is different. It is absolutely and clearly established that there is no ideal style that fits all, or even most, situations. This has been demonstrated conclusively and I write from 30 years' experience of looking into it.

About cheating: do not cheat on these tests unless lying is one of your strong points. As the older politician replied to the younger politician in response to the question 'How can one be effective as a politician?'; 'Be absolutely sincere, honest and candid . . . if you can fake that you can fake anything'. Obviously that is not the game.

As you go through the book you will see that I make many attempts to get you to share your results with others, even to get others to complete the book as well. This is not a selling exercise on my part. It is in an effort to help you to discuss results with others – both your results and theirs – so that you can share your perceptions and misconceptions and hopefully increase your self-awareness. Why not go for it? You may have a training section in your organization. If you like this book then get a key trainer to complete it and ask whether that trainer thinks it would be good to be used on a wider basis. No, this is not a selling exercise – it is a *helpful* exercise.

Clearly this book is intended for managers. Most managers know little of the details of test construction and really do not want to. This has been my direct experience in over 35 years of working with thousands of managers on tests. However, some general background is always useful. I quite deliberately did not make these comments a separate chapter as I wanted to put emphasis on increasing your self-awareness rather than on your becoming pseudo-psychometricians. One very popular defence known to psychologists is intellectualization. Some people do not like their test results. They then ask a whole series of questions such as: 'how many millions of managers have taken it?'; 'has it been approved by every psychological association in the world?'; 'have the validity tests been exhaustive?' and so on . . . I do not want to help you get into that kind of fix.

Tests are commonly used for feedback and some are used for assessment. They are usually administered on an individual basis and are most often used for selection purposes although no mention is made of it in this book. The whole idea behind this book, and I have been relentless with the idea, is that the tests here are best used for feedback to the individual so that the individual may improve self-awareness and thus improve effectiveness. The way I am proposing that these tests be used is to be helpful, not to play 'gotcha'.

This book contains a fairly wide variety of test types. The Management Human Relations Test, for instance, has absolutely no right or wrong answers. The test is what we call purely attitudinal. It shows what you think about people. This is where norms become very important, because if you score five percentile on that, it means that you certainly have a more negative attitude towards people than 90 per cent of other managers. On the XYZ Inventory, again, there are no right or wrong answers. The test indicates your views about the nature of other people. Some tests are meant to be fairly definitive in terms of what is best. These include Communication Knowledge Inventory, Management Change Inventory, and Management Coaching Relations Tests. Test designers obviously have their own biases and so right and wrong are certainly hard to prove. However, as before, if you do score 5 percentile, you know what it means.

Where appropriate, which is in most cases, the tests in this book have been *normed*. What this means, in essence, is that the test is given to a group of managers, usually as diverse a group as possible, so that managers who complete the test can compare themselves in terms of 'high' and 'low' to other managers. There are many tests now available for managers which are not normed, so you really do not know what your scores mean unless you want to take the test designer's word for it. This is not true for the tests in this book. Where appropriate the tests here have been normed on a wide variety and a sufficient quantity of managers. For example, the Management Coaching Relations Test was normed on 1,895 managers. So if you score 95 percentile on that test, it means you are in the top 10 per cent of a diverse group of managers. If you score five percentile it means you are in the lowest ten per cent. Norming is critically important if you are to make any realistic interpretation of how you compare with other managers.

Test reliability indicates the degree to which, if the test is done again by the same manager in the same situation, the results are similar. This is a fairly important concept because if a test does not agree with itself, it cannot agree with anything else. Reliability correlations run from 0 to 1.0. For example, on one test (not included here) reliability runs from 0.71 to 0.93 on the various scales. This was based on testing 107 managers at one point in time and then two months later while they were still in the same job. This level of reliability is quite satisfactory for the way tests are being used in this book. If, to a degree, a test measures behaviour rather than straight personality, and if the manager completes the test again perhaps a year later in a different situation, then one would naturally expect reliabilities to drop. If they remain very high, one would suspect the manager of rigidity. This point of view is not understood by some who believe that every test is a personality test and the higher the reliability the better, in every case.

When tests are used in training and development, it is established that face validity is a key issue. That is, does the average manager, on looking at the test items, think that they more or less measure what the test claims to measure? All of the tests in this book have very high face validity. They appear accurate to a manager who is asked to complete them.

If you want further information on the norming, reliability, or validity of any of these tests, please write to Organizational Tests (Canada) Ltd and ask for a fact sheet. I could have included such information in this book but, again, it would lure the book away from its central purpose which is to increase self-awareness in order to improve effectiveness. Fact sheets are not available for all tests, as for some they are inappropriate (the Time Usage Diary for example). The other way to learn more about this subject is to attend the course designed especially for trainers, which is outlined in Chapter 19.

Several of the tests here are from Organizational Tests Limited (OTL), who own the copyright. This firm sells tests, primarily in North America but also in other countries. They generously provided tests for this book, but they urged that readers should not photocopy them and pass them around the office. If you wish to have additional tests, please write for their catalogue to: *Organizational Tests Limited, PO Box 324, Fredericton, New Brunswick, Canada E3B 4Y9.*

There are two parts of this book that you are free to photocopy – by having this freedom you will be better able to discuss your results with others. The two parts are Chapter 15 which gives a profile of your scores, and Chapter 16 which gives the scale definitions and descriptions. *Please do not photocopy other parts.* Either buy more books or buy the individual tests. Information on how to access individual tests is given in Chapter 20.

W. J. Reddin Ph.D.
PO Box 1012
Fredericton
New Brunswick
E3B 5B4
Canada

Thanks To . . .

I would like to thank the following numerous people and organizations:

First, Valerie Richardson for her support.

John Fry, who managed the book from start to finish and who came up with many useful ideas, pointed out several sexist statements and, in many ways, certainly made the book more useful.

Charlie Chambre, who managed Organizational Tests Limited for more than 20 years and thus helped the tests in this book to have wider currency, better norms and much better documentation.

Laura Hasselman, who is now manager of Organizational Tests Limited.

Val Barratt, Sylvia Davis, Marion Platt and Glynis Taplin, who typed and retyped and organized and reorganized the various drafts with care.

Organizational Tests Limited, who have the copyrights for all these tests and allowed me to use them in this book form.

Abraham Maslow, for his brilliant model of human growth and development, mainly concerning self-actualization, on which the self-actualization inventory is partly based.

Douglas McGregor, the warm-hearted mentor of mine during his last days at MIT who so successfully shocked the world, and particularly industrial America, with his theory that things do not have to be run in an autocratic method. It is on his ideas that the XYZ inventory is based.

Keith Stewart, who co-developed with me the four tests in Chapters 4, 5, 7 and 8.

Ken Rowell, who co-developed with me the tests in Chapters 6 and 8.

Brian Sullivan, who co-developed with me the test in Chapter 9.

In particular I wish to acknowledge the co-operation and support of those organizations who used one or more of these tests as an approach to organizational change, and to thank them for advancing these ideas, for making them even more practical, and for being willing to share their information and experiences. My thanks to:

Arthur Young
Atlas Air
Bowater Scott
Ethiopian Airlines
Falconbridge Nickel Mines
Ford Motor Company
General Motors
IBM Corporation
International Computers Limited
John Player & Son
Johnson Wax
Metal Box
Moosehead Breweries
New Brunswick Electric Power Commission
Pedigree Petfood
Siemens
Westinghouse
Westpac Banking Corporation
US Civil Service Commission.

Part I: This Book and You

This first part sets out the benefits of the book and how to use it.

If a man has a talent and cannot use it, he has failed. If he has a talent and uses one half of it he has partly failed. If he has a talent and learns somehow to use the whole of it, he has gloriously succeeded and won a satisfaction and triumph few men will know.

Thomas Wolfe

One of the great differences between the amateur and the professional is that the latter has the capacity to progress.

W. Somerset Maugham

Chapter 1

How This Book
Will Benefit You

INTRODUCTION

This book can provide you with many benefits. The central one is self-awareness but there are many other associated benefits. We all have different personalities and needs. Because we all learn differently and are employed in different types of work, obviously more value will be obtained from some parts of this book than from others.

BENEFITS

Some of the benefits you may gain from this book are outlined below.

Increasing your self-awareness

Self-change, and change in others, must start with self-awareness. If you do not know where you stand, how can you truly evaluate where others are? If you think you are a heavily oriented relationships manager when in fact you are a heavily oriented task manager this will cause you much confusion and lead you to do the wrong things and to interpret things incorrectly. We do not have to go back to Socrates who wrote 'Know thyself' but it is not a bad place to start. In this book your self-awareness will be increased sharply through a variety of means.

Increasing your situational sensitivity

Once you have a better idea of where you are you can easily improve your ability to read situations for what they really contain. Some people distort. They bring a lot of ideas to every situation and recite these ideas rather than read the situation. People are different and situations are different. There are many popular forms of distortion and you may see yourself in one or more of them as they are described in this book.

Lowering your job stress

Hundreds of scientific studies have been conducted into the causes of stress at work. There are many causes and most are obvious. They include such things as the general level of job dissatisfaction, poor relationships with superiors or others, belief that the job is of little value, not understanding the job, not having the resources to do the job well, lack of recognition, and undue time pressure. Some of these occur in our jobs for all of us at times. They can be greatly decreased, however, with the help of the many ideas in this book. The problem is not just work stress but what work stress can lead to. High work stress has been related to a variety of physical ailments, particularly heart disease, arthritis and peptic ulcers.

Working smarter, not harder

Working harder does not necessarily mean becoming more effective. This book may well lead you to think, reflect and plan more, rather than putting more hours in or slavishly 'doing' when you should be thinking about being smart.

A less effective manager of a purchasing function worked very hard, worrying a lot, always taking work home at night, and sometimes putting in work at the weekends. This manager was told by the team members – and this was supported by a consultant working with the team –

that the manager 'worked too hard'. This was highly offensive and was taken as a personal insult.

This manager could not see the wood for the trees and did not want to – it would mean that behaviour would have to change, by having to sit and think about the job and having to delegate more. It was change that was frightening and this was hidden by saying that 'one had to work hard'. A popular defence for less effective managers is that 'my job demands that I put in long hours'. In some particular situations that may be true in the short term. Most jobs, however, are designed to be done in normal working hours, not excessively long hours.

A manager's true worth to the company may sometimes be measured by the amount of time that person could remain dead in the office without anyone noticing. The longer the time, the more likely it is that the manager makes long-run policy decisions rather than short-run administrative decisions. The key decisions in a company are long-run and may refer to market entry, new product introduction, new plant location, or key appointments. The person making these should not get involved, as can happen, with short-run issues. If that should be the case, the manager has not decided on the output measures of the job or does not have the skill or opportunity to create conditions where only policy issues reach that level. Work smarter, not harder.

POTENTIAL BENEFITS

The potential benefits that this book can provide for you are discussed below.

Advancing your own management development

In various ways this book provides you with a comprehensive management development programme. One part of this is the learning you will obtain as a result of completing the tests. Quite a different part, and equally important, is the selection of actions you will take as a result of making the decisions discussed in Chapter 17.

Action steps to improve your effectiveness

Chapter 17 provides 38 action steps which can lead to your improving your effectiveness. It all takes time but all the steps are relatively straightforward to engage, if you wish to do so. Those who truly want to increase their effectiveness and spend some time on it will take that chapter very seriously and complete many of the action steps proposed.

Obtaining a coaching framework

Several of the tests in this book used individually, or the book used as a whole, provide you with an excellent coaching framework for your subordinates. A good way to approach this is to give one or all of your subordinates the book to complete. Share your results with them and offer to talk about any of their test results that they care to show you. If you want greatly to improve open and easy communication with your subordinates – that is the way.

Others knowing you better

Sharing your test results with others will lead directly to their knowing and understanding you far better than they would have thought possible. You, obviously, select who the 'others' are. There are many suggestions for this in Chapter 17. These 'others' might be your superior, your spouse, your children, your subordinates, or strangers on a seminar who, possibly by taking a more detached view, may be even greater help to you in thinking about changes you could make to improve your effectiveness.

Knowing others better

This is the reverse of the previous point. Use the tests in this book and get to know others. A key principle, of course, would be sharing your results with them.

Improving your selection skill

This book is not written around the concept of using tests for selection. It is written around the concept of using tests for self-awareness and self-development. However, as you get to know the tests better it is fairly certain you will think that some fit certain jobs in your organization quite well. As an extreme example, some jobs in your organization are highly bureaucratic, are designed that way and, perhaps, have to be that way. Probably you would not want to hire someone for such a job who scored near the bottom on the bureaucratic scales. Certain jobs require certain values.

Increasing your diagnostic skill

The tests in this book can lead directly to your greatly increasing your diagnostic skill with individuals, teams, situations and organizations.

All the tests have a clear individual application. All are useful to discuss on a team basis when the individual is being discussed. Some of the tests are particularly suited to looking at a team as a whole or an organization as a whole; that is, when the test results are added for a team or an organization they still make sense.

RATING THE RELATIVE BENEFITS TO YOU

Which of these benefits are most important to you?

- Review the following seven possible benefits to you from using this book.

- Indicate for each the ones which, for you, have a high (H), average (A) or low (L) benefit.

Advancing your own management development	H A L
Action steps to improve your effectiveness	H A L
Obtaining a coaching framework	H A L
Others knowing you better	H A L
Knowing others better	H A L
Improving your selection skill	H A L
Increasing your diagnostic skill	H A L

- Obviously you are highly motivated to obtain the benefits you have rated as (H). This book can be of great assistance to you in obtaining all of those benefits.

God gives the nuts, but He does not crack them.

Proverb

Don't be afraid to take a big step if one is indicated. You can't cross a chasm in two small jumps.

David Lloyd George

Appetite comes with eating.

Rabelais

Chapter 2

How to Use This Book

INTRODUCTION

Here are some ideas for you on how to use this book. Some books are designed to be read chapter by chapter in the sequence presented – this one is not. I propose a great variety of methods for using this book. Use those that motivate you most.

SUGGESTED METHODS

Overview the book

It might be a good idea for you to flip over the book, page by page, to get a general impression of what it contains. This will help you to make your own judgement about some of the other ideas that follow. It would be good to get a sniff of what the tests measure and, from Chapters 14 and 17, how these can relate to your work and general situation.

Complete the tests in any order

Each of the 11 tests stands independently of the others. If you wish, start with any one that interests you. The interpretation of each test is given in the test chapter and, for the majority, a comparison of your score to other managers. Dip in as you wish.

Estimated time for completion

The time for completion varies widely from individual to individual. A shorter time to complete is no better than a longer time to complete. Plan on anything from 5 to 20 hours.

Give the book to others now

Before you start on any of the tests it might be a good idea for you to discuss the book with colleagues. Tell them you have not completed any test and that you have no idea how you might score, but if they are 'in' you are also 'in' and this could be followed up by a one-day meeting where you discuss all your scores. In some situations where the trust level is a little low you will not get anywhere. In others it will be the natural thing to do.

Using the book only for your personal development

While this book will nudge you to discuss your results with others this is not necessary for enabling you to benefit from the book. You will have to decide after you complete it whether your results should be shared and whether you want others to share their results with you. This book stands very well on its own as a statement from you about yourself.

Do not lie unless it is one of your real strengths

Obviously you will answer every test to the best of your ability. We can all be very hard on ourselves or very easy on ourselves – it is the balance that counts. Be fair to the test and fair to yourself to get a balanced result.

Self-awareness or action plan

The 11 tests will quite definitely increase your self-awareness. This is the thrust of the book for you. The higher benefits can be obtained by doing something about your increased self-awareness; ideas on how you might do this are included in Chapter 14. You will have to make a balanced judgement as to whether your increased self-awareness is the start or the end point.

Complete this on a trip

This is a good book to take along with you on a plane or train trip – the longer the journey the better. It has also been found successful to complete it while on holiday. Give some thought to when and where you will work on it.

Part II: Test Chapters

This main part of the book consists of the 11 tests which are the basis for the output-oriented manager's insights.

Physical science helps us to describe, explain, predict and control the physical world. Management science must do just the same for organizations.

WJR

Information is at least the lubricant of the business and may be its heart.

WJR

It isn't what you know that counts, it's what you think of in time.

Unknown

Chapter 3

Communication Knowledge Inventory

INTRODUCTION

The Communication Knowledge Inventory is a test of general communication knowledge for managers.

Some statements contain communication fallacies, comprising misconceptions of both verbal and non-verbal communication. Other statements demonstrate the principles of verbal communication and verbal methods of expressing thoughts, feelings and factual data. There are also statements on non-verbal methods of expressing thoughts and feelings.

INSTRUCTIONS FOR ANSWERING

Decide whether you believe each of the statements is either true (T) or false (F) by circling the appropriate letter.

COMMUNICATION KNOWLEDGE INVENTORY

1. Humour most often serves to relieve tension at a meeting.   T   F

2. The people who suggest 'Let's appoint a Chairman' very often want to be appointed themselves.   T   F

---

3. Doodling usually aids listening.   T   F

4. People don't like to listen to or read about things they disagree with.   T   F

5. Rumours are never worth listening to.   T   F

6. Communication is a simple process.   T   F

7. People who do not listen are usually not interested.   T   F

8. When people won't stop talking, it is usually because they have a lot of important information to give.   T   F

9. People usually forget things which do not interest them.   T   F

10. The way a person stands is an important form of communication.   T   F

11. Listening well comes naturally.   T   F

12. Talking convincingly is one of the most important skills a person should have to ensure effective communication.   T   F

13. When feelings are hurt, effective communication has not taken place.   T   F

14. A smile does not always indicate pleasure.   T   F

15. The first person arriving at a meeting is often the most interested.   T   F

16. While it might be a kind thing to do, it makes little real sense to encourage quiet people in a group to speak more.   T   F

17. The people who are the easiest to convince are nearly always the ones who are able to understand the quickest.   T   F

18. Clothes reflect personality.   T   F

19. A person who knows a subject well can nearly always communicate it well.   T   F

20. The person who sits at the head of the table at a meeting may be trying to dominate.   T F

21. The way a word is spoken affects its meaning.   T F

22. When people fear criticism, they are likely to talk less.   T F

23. Silence can most usually be interpreted as agreement.   T F

24. The person who talks the most is probably trying to dominate.   T F

25. Misunderstandings are seldom caused by the meaning of a word.   T F

26. Anger is usually expressed best by raising the voice.   T F

27. People usually communicate better when they are in a good mood.   T F

28. Outgoing people are much more likely to communicate effectively than quiet people.   T F

29. When people are angry, they often talk less.　　T　F

30. The people sitting farthest from the table can be indicating that they are the least interested.　　T　F

31. If an instruction is clearly understood it will nearly always be carried out.　　T　F

32. Just listening to problems does little good unless you can later offer the person some advice.　　T　F

33. Shouting at someone never does any good.　　T　F

34. Leaning back in a chair can indicate disinterest.　　T　F

35. Glancing often at one's watch in a meeting probably indicates a desire to leave the meeting.　　T　F

36. A person in a group who keeps suggesting different ways of doing things only slows the group down and makes it less effective.　　T　F

37. Stating a point loudly and frequently is usually the most effective way to get it across.　　T　F

38. Gazing around while someone else is talking probably indicates disinterest in what is being said.   T   F

39. People who say less have less to offer.   T   F

40. A person who offers to go to the board or chart at a meeting may be trying to dominate.   T   F

41. Anger can be expressed in such a way that the receiver will understand and accept it.   T   F

42. Fear of embarrassment may make people say they understand when they do not.   T   F

43. The total responsibility for effective communication is on the person who is talking.   T   F

44. The feeling expressed in a communication may be more important than the actual words used.   T   F

45. Intelligent people should understand a message the first time.   T   F

46. A heated argument is usually an indication that clear communication is taking place.   T   F

47. A slip of the tongue such as using a wrong word may reveal true feelings.　　T　F

48. Effective communication seldom takes place between people who are arguing.　　T　F

49. Raising the voice may indicate enthusiasm.　　T　F

50. A person's facial expression can change the meaning of the words spoken.　　T　F

51. A person who asks a lot of questions does not understand as clearly as a person who asks a few.　　T　F

52. When people do not understand a message, they will nearly always tell you so.　　T　F

53. Arguments should be avoided at meetings.　　T　F

54. Nodding the head up and down while listening usually indicates interest.　　T　F

55. Raising one's eyebrows can make another person stop talking.　　T　F

56. A forceful person seldom persuades others to say they agree when they really do not.   T   F

57. People with large vocabularies are much more likely to communicate effectively.   T   F

58. The last person arriving at a meeting is often the least interested.   T   F

59. Whenever possible, information should be communicated verbally rather than in written form.   T   F

60. The objects in a person's room can tell you something about that individual's personality.   T   F

61. Repeating what a person has said is a good check to see if the message was understood properly.   T   F

62. A misspelled word can sometimes reveal more than the same word spelled correctly.   T   F

63. No news is good news.   T   F

64. Listening without saying anything can be very helpful in itself.   T   F

65. Written communication is always more effective than verbal communication.   T F

66. A quiet person is less likely to understand a message than a person who asks questions about it.   T F

67. Effective communication only takes place when the receiver understands the message the way the sender intended it.   T F

68. People who are strangers are likely to communicate as effectively as people who know each other.   T F

69. People who really disagree may say they agree only to avoid further argument.   T F

70. People often communicate without realizing it.   T F

71. The meaning of communication does not usually change as it is passed on to other people.   T F

72. Correct spelling is important for written communication.   T F

73. The person who speaks the most in a group is nearly always the most effective member.   T   F

74. The way a person shakes your hand reflects the person's personality.   T   F

75. Sometimes even slight gestures mean as much as words.   T   F

76. A group in which only a few disagreements arise is more effective than a group in which many disagreements arise.   T   F

77. All important communication is either written or verbal.   T   F

78. The books a person reads can indicate much about that individual's personality.   T   F

79. Moving the hands while talking usually hinders effective communication.   T   F

80. Different people communicate similar feelings in different ways.   T   F

HOW TO CALCULATE YOUR SCORE

Section A: Communication fallacies

If you answered any of these statements as false, circle the number and then add up the total number of circles in this section.

  3,   5,   6,   8, 11, 12, 13, 16, 17, 19,

23, 25, 26, 28, 31, 32, 33, 36, 37, 39,

43, 45, 46, 48, 51, 52, 53, 56, 57, 59,

63, 65, 66, 68, 71, 72, 73, 76, 77, 79.

Total for Section A . . . .

The correct answer to all of these is 'false'. They all concern popular misconceptions about verbal and non-verbal communication.

Section B: Verbal communication

If you answered any of these statements as true, circle the number and then add up the total number of circles in this section.

1, 2, 4, 7, 9, 21, 22, 24, 27, 29,

41, 42, 44, 47, 49, 61, 62, 64, 67, 69.

Total for Section B . . . .

The correct answer to all of these is 'true'.

Section C: Non-verbal communication

If you answered any of these statements as true, circle the number and then add up the total number of circles in this section.

10, 14, 15, 18, 20, 30, 34, 35, 38, 40,

50, 54, 55, 58, 60, 70, 74, 75, 78, 80.

Total for Section C . . . .

The correct answer to all of these is 'true'.

Grand Total (Sections A, B and C) . . . .
(maximum 80)

HOW DO YOU COMPARE WITH OTHERS?

To compare yourself with 648 other managers, identify your score below and read above it for the adjusted category (such as Very low VL). Circle one category below.

Very low VL	Low L	Average ME	High H	Very high VH
Up to 54	55–57	58–60	61–63	64–80

PROFILE CHART

Communication *Knowledge* *Inventory*	Very low VL	Low L	Aver- age ME	High H	Very high VH

Shade or hatch in your adjusted category from the above section on 'How do you compare with others?' This will be used again for your overall profile in Chapter 15.

I once asked a farmer for directions to a neighbouring village and he told me, 'You can't get there from here'. I sometimes run into the same problem with senior managers with change objectives.

WJR

The Situationist's Prayer
Give me the serenity to accept what cannot be changed,
The courage to change what should be changed,
And the wisdom to distinguish one from the other.

St Francis

There is nothing more difficult to take in hand, more perilous to conduct, or more uncertain in its success, than to take the lead in the introduction of a new order of things.

Machiavelli

INTRODUCTION

The Management Change Inventory is an 80-question true/false test of knowledge or attitudes toward management principles and practices concerning change. It will indicate your approach towards change introduction compared to a particular point of view.

INSTRUCTIONS FOR ANSWERING

Read each statement and indicate your answer by circling either T (true) or F (false).

You may find it difficult to make up your mind about some statements. However, in every case circle either T or F.

MANAGEMENT CHANGE INVENTORY

1. If managers cannot size up situations, they will usually introduce change clumsily.　　T　F

2. Employees will be more likely to accept change if they can have some influence over the nature and direction of it.　　T　F

---

3. Employees often resist change because they do not understand the objectives of it.   T   F

4. Group discussion is seldom a good way to introduce change.   T   F

5. Talks on the nature of the world in the year 2100 are a good way to lower resistance to change   T   F

6. Employees are more likely to accept change if their ideas on improvements are listened to and used.   T   F

7. No changes at all will lead to greater long-run stability than change itself.   T   F

8. Change is introduced best if there is a complete understanding about its end objectives.   T   F

9. Most conflict between managers is caused by differences in personality.   T   F

10. Resistance to change is lower if managers keep the drawbacks of the change to themselves.   T   F

11. Once a change has been announced the maximum possible information should be distributed concerning it.   T   F

12. Employees are more likely to accept change if they know management is committed to the change.   T   F

13. Some changes are easier to accept if they are announced in a formal manner.   T   F

14. A well developed plan on paper is only a short step to the plan well implemented.   T   F

15. People will be more likely to change if their personality problems are explained to them.   T   F

16. Supervisors are more likely to accept new managers if formal meetings or ceremonies are used to introduce them.   T   F

17. Change can sometimes be initially proposed with a suggestion of discipline for resistance to it.   T   F

18. Change is usually resisted if it is seen as being based on personal ambitions.   T   F

19. Change should always be introduced slowly.   T   F

20. The notice board is usually a good way to announce change.   T   F

21. Employees are more likely to accept change if they are dealt with honestly.   T   F

22. A discussion of the method of introducing the change is often as useful as a discussion of the change itself.   T   F

23. There comes a point where a manager may have to stop all discussion about a change and simply introduce it.   T   F

24. Those who resist change are generally not interested in the change one way or the other.   T   F

25. Subordinates will be more likely to accept change if only the positive aspects of it are mentioned.   T   F

26. When a change is resisted the manager who actually introduces it is often at fault.   T   F

27. Slow introduction of a change usually produces greater resistance to it.　　T　F

28. Supervisors work better if their manager discusses their performance with them.　　T　F

29. The more technically skilled supervisors usually introduce change best.　　T　F

30. Employees are more likely to resist change if they know the real reason behind it.　　T　F

31. An often unstated question about a proposed change is 'How will this affect me?'　　T　F

32. Employees work better if they receive rewards for their extra effort.　　T　F

33. Most organizations must change with the times in order to survive.　　T　F

34. It is an easy matter to implement changes in rules and procedures.　　T　F

35. Changes in company policy should never be discussed in advance of their introduction.   T   F

36. A good argument for rapid change is that the worker would have a shorter uncomfortable period of adjustment.   T   F

37. Change is introduced best if there is little prior discussion about it.   T   F

38. Change is introduced best if as much time is spent on planning the introduction of it as there is on introducing it.   T   F

39. Most changes lead to higher productivity immediately.   T   F

40. Managers resist change less than supervisors do.   T   F

41. Employees work better if they are well informed.   T   F

42. Employees will be likely to accept change when they are able to influence it even slightly.   T   F

43. When introducing change, management should tell supervision and employees virtually everything concerning it.   T   F

44. An increase in wages is probably the best way to reduce resistance to change.　　　　　　　　　T　F

45. The introduction of a change need not be planned.　　　　　　　　T　F

46. Managers introduce change best if they consider each situation as different and handle it accordingly.　　T　F

47. All change benefits the employee, the supervisor, and the company.　　　T　F

48. Employees often resist change because of fear of the unknown.　　T　F

49. Slow introduction of change lessens understanding about it.　　　　　　T　F

50. Participation must involve acceptance by management of employees' suggestions.　　　　　　　　　T　F

51. Employees should be informed in advance of changes that will affect them.　　　　　　　　　　T　F

52. Subordinates often resist change because they have been comfortable with the current situation.　　T　F

53. Change will be more likely to lead to increased productivity if those affected participate in advance concerning the change.   T F

54. Changes are best introduced by the personnel department.   T F

55. Resistance to change is usually greatest at the worker level.   T F

56. It is often easier to change a group than to change an individual.   T F

57. Everyone understands what participative management means.   T F

58. Change will usually be resisted if it is seen as a personal idea of the manager.   T F

59. It is generally easier to change your superior than to change your subordinate.   T F

60. Resistance to a change is increased if those most affected by it are informed in advance.   T F

61. If subordinates are told the reason for a change, they will be more likely to accept it.   T F

62. Managers should be evaluated in a large part by their ability to introduce change smoothly.   T   F

63. Employees usually resist change because they do not understand enough about it.   T   F

64. A manager need only announce what changes are planned to be made and not how they are to be implemented.   T   F

65. Change is introduced best if employees are first taught why they resist change.   T   F

66. Whenever possible those affected should be allowed to plan the rate at which a change is introduced.   T   F

67. Managers should write as many of their communications as they can.   T   F

68. Change is introduced best if a plan of introduction is followed.   T   F

69. Managers who introduce change should pay particular attention to the technical rather than the human aspects of the change.   T   F

70. Important changes are always best introduced by written memo.   T   F

71. People work best if they have a say in the way they do their work.   T   F

72. Many experiments show that if employees are allowed to set their own output level, they set a higher level than their manager would.   T   F

73. Change sometimes must be introduced on the basis of 'We will do this if you do that'.   T   F

74. Staff specialists should have the responsibility and authority for introducing changes in line departments.   T   F

75. Resistance to change is almost always emotional not rational.   T   F

76. Most changes should begin at the top and work down the organization structure.   T   F

77. Employees should not be involved in planning the method of introducing changes.   T   F

78. Group discussion can be useful in keeping those with minority views in line.   T   F

79. Participation is a sound way to sell workers on an idea about which management has already made a decision.   T   F

80. The introduction of change is not an important management function.   T   F

HOW TO CALCULATE YOUR SCORE

If you answered an item as true and it is listed below as true, then circle that number. If you answered an item as false and it is listed below under false, then circle that number.

True	False
1 2 3 6 8 11 12 13	4 5 7 9 10 14 15 17
16 18 21 22 23 26 28 31	19 20 24 25 27 29 30 34
32 33 36 38 41 42 43 46	35 37 39 40 44 45 47 49
48 51 52 53 56 58 61 62	50 54 55 57 59 60 64 65
63 66 68 71 72 73 76 78	67 69 70 74 75 77 79 80

Total true ....   Total false ....

Total the circles from *both* true and false – this is your total raw score.

Total raw score ....

HOW DO YOU COMPARE WITH OTHERS?

To compare yourself with other managers, use the table below. This test is based on international norms of 1,895 managers. Identify your total raw score then read the adjusted category above it. An adjusted category of 5 means that you are in the lowest 5 per cent of managers in introducing change based on the principles of this test. A score of 75 or more means that you are in the top 25 per cent or so. A higher adjusted category indicates higher change introduction effectiveness than a lower one.

Adjusted category:	5	15	25	35	45	55	65	75	85	95
Total raw scores:	0–52	53–54	55–56	57–58	59–60	61–62	63–64	65–66	67–68	69–80

PROFILE CHART

Percentile

Management Change Inventory	5	15	25	35	45	55	65	75	85	95

Shade or hatch in your adjusted category from the above section on 'How do you compare with others?' This will be used again for your overall profile in Chapter 15.

WHAT IS BEING MEASURED?

What is being measured by this test is the extent to which you have knowledge of sound methods of introducing change. It may or may not fit you or your situation at the moment but it does seem to fit many others. It cannot be argued, of course, that all the statements the test claims to be true are, in fact, true and all the statements the test claims to be false are, in fact, false. However, it can be said that by and large the statements taken as a whole do reflect what the test measures. You can check the assumption in the test yourself by simply referring to each statement and see whether the test claims it is generally true or generally false. The following statements give an idea of what is believed to be true.

- Employees often resist change because they do not understand the objectives of it.

- Once a change has been announced the maximum possible information should be distributed concerning it.

- Employees are more likely to accept change if they know management is committed to the change.

- Change is usually resisted if it is seen as being based on personal ambitions.

- Employees work better if they receive rewards for their extra effort.

- Most organizations must change with the times in order to survive.

- Change is introduced best if as much time is spent on planning the introduction of it as there is on introducing it.

- Employees work better if they are well informed.

- Employees should be informed in advance of changes that will affect them.

- It is often easier to change a group than to change an individual.

- Managers should be evaluated in a large part by their ability to introduce change smoothly.

- Whenever possible those affected should be allowed to plan the rate at which a change is introduced.

- Change is introduced best if a plan of introduction is followed.

- People work best if they have a say in the way they do their work.

- Employees often resist change because of fear of the unknown.

This Inventory was developed by W. J. Reddin and E. K. Stewart

Too many management development programmes appear to be designed to ravish the retina while leaving the mind untouched.

WJR

Young managers should not be trained by those who have ceased to learn.

WJR

If he is indeed wise, he does not bid you enter the house of his own wisdom; but rather leads you to the threshold of your own mind.

Kahlil Gibran

Chapter 5

Management Coaching Relations Test

INTRODUCTION

The Management Coaching Relations Test is a test of your knowledge of sound methods of coaching your team members, who themselves may be managers. The topics covered include: performance appraisal, effectiveness criteria, coaching interview and training. This test is jargon free and it emphasizes principles and common sense rather than theory.

INSTRUCTIONS FOR ANSWERING

Read each statement and indicate your answer by circling either T (true) or F (false).

You may find it difficult to make up your mind about some statements. However, in every case circle either T or F.

MANAGEMENT COACHING RELATIONS TEST

1. A manager should listen closely to a subordinate even though the discussion leaves the point occasionally.　　T　F

2. Coaching often results in a more relaxed and productive work atmosphere.　　T　F

---

3. Subordinates asking for advice should make appointments in advance.　　　T　F

4. It is unwise to mention evidence of poor performance during a coaching session.　　　T　F

5. Coaching is more effective if it is scheduled on an annual basis.　　　T　F

6. It is best if managers know both their subordinates' strengths and weaknesses.　　　T　F

7. Coaching should not include discussions on personal cleanliness and hygiene.　　　T　F

8. Managers should coach their subordinates not only on work skills but on human skills as well.　　　T　F

9. Coaching is not a continuing part of a manager's job.　　　T　F

10. In most successful coaching situations the manager talks most.　　　T　F

11. A prime objective of coaching is to bring out all the reasons for poor performance.　　　　　　T　F

12. Subordinates will talk more if the manager really listens to what is said.　　　　　　T　F

13. Coaching and appraisal sessions should be held at different times.　　　　　　T　F

14. Disagreement should be avoided at coaching sessions.　　　　　　T　F

15. Subordinates will talk more if the manager shows interest by writing down parts of the discussion.　　　　　　T　F

16. Training in human relations would help a manager become a better coach.　　　　　　T　F

17. Most people have similar backgrounds and should be treated alike.　　　　　　T　F

18. The first step in effective coaching is to put the other person at ease.　　　　　　T　F

19. Good listeners often doodle while
    someone is talking to them.   T   F

20. A coaching session is more effective
    when the manager maintains the
    position as boss.   T   F

21. Coaching should be handled by the
    manager whenever possible.   T   F

22. If managers cannot size up people
    their coaching will be poor.   T   F

23. The usefulness of coaching is often
    increased when the session is held
    outside the regular work area.   T   F

24. Tape recordings of coaching ses-
    sions are useful for personnel de-
    partment records.   T   F

25. The success of coaching is usually
    increased when a third person is
    present.   T   F

26. Productivity will usually increase if a
    subordinate feels free to talk to the
    manager in confidence.   T   F

27. Coaching and counselling should be
    left to experts.   T   F

28. When coaching, a manager must show a willingness to see the employee's point of view. T F

29. If it has not been written into the job description a manager should not be too concerned with coaching. T F

30. Subordinates should be kept a bit on edge in coaching sessions so they will talk more. T F

31. A common cause of low productivity is a person in the wrong job. T F

32. All managers should be good at coaching. T F

33. Watching a subordinate's face during coaching sessions will increase understanding. T F

34. A smile always indicates pleasure. T F

35. All coaching should be done sitting down. T F

36. A manager could spend almost full time at coaching and be very effective. T F

37. Disciplinary action usually precedes a coaching session.   T   F

38. Subordinates can sometimes solve problems themselves if they have the opportunity to talk to others.   T   F

39. Usually only one coaching session is all that is required.   T   F

40. The most important skill a manager should have to ensure good coaching is to talk convincingly.   T   F

41. People often communicate similar feelings in different ways.   T   F

42. Leaning back in a chair can indicate disinterest.   T   F

43. Effective coaching is often achieved over a cup of coffee.   T   F

44. The best end result of a coaching session is that the manager gets the subordinate to do things the company's way.   T   F

45. It is easier to converse with a person sitting opposite you at a table than one sitting next to you.   T   F

46. A manager can show interest in what is being said by nodding the head.　　T　F

47. If an employee appears unsettled during a coaching session it is best to ignore it.　　T　F

48. In many successful coaching situations the coach may do nothing more than nod the head.　　T　F

49. A coaching session is the best place for a subordinate to get something off the chest.　　T　F

50. Subordinates should never be advised to resign if they are performing satisfactorily.　　T　F

51. Coaching is essentially a helping relationship.　　T　F

52. Coaching is best when it is informal.　　T　F

53. People can be helped best when they really want help.　　T　F

54. Coaching is essentially telling people what to do.　　T　F

55. Regular written reports should be given to managers on their performance.   T   F

56. Coaching is less effective if always initiated by managers.   T   F

57. Managers should give advice concerning any personal problems brought to them.   T   F

58. A worker should never be criticized in front of co-workers.   T   F

59. Sarcasm should be used occasionally with specific subordinates if the manager wishes to improve their behaviour.   T   F

60. A prime objective of coaching is to improve a subordinate's personality.   T   F

61. The quality of coaching will increase as honesty and frankness increase.   T   F

62. Coaching is best if concerned only with on-the-job behaviour.   T   F

63. A good manager listens more than talks.   T   F

64. A table to sit at makes coaching more effective.　　　　　　T　F

65. One of the chief objectives of coaching is to make a subordinate feel better.　　　　　　T　F

66. Coaching is very difficult if the subordinate does not see the need for assistance.　　　　　　T　F

67. Managers should not try to appear generally helpful as it would make them appear soft-hearted.　　　　　　T　F

68. Coaching is best when the employee decides the way to improve performance.　　　　　　T　F

69. Coaching is not as effective as just telling a subordinate how to do the job.　　　　　　T　F

70. The best coaching is followed up by a written note.　　　　　　T　F

71. A coaching session is far less effective when interruptions occur.　　　　　　T　F

72. The main objective of coaching is to improve productivity.　　　　　　T　F

73. Coaching, counselling, giving friendly advice, and helping mean much the same thing.   T F

74. The manager should always use a formal step-by-step procedure in a coaching session.   T F

75. It is primarily the personnel department's job to give advice on how best to improve performance.   T F

76. It is difficult to be a coach and a judge at the same time.   T F

77. Coaching is essentially a corrective-type interview.   T F

78. Subordinates will talk more if the manager shows interest by appropriate comments.   T F

79. Coaching is always more effective when the manager is a personal friend of the subordinate.   T F

80. Long periods of silence in a coaching session usually means it is not going too well.   T F

HOW TO CALCULATE YOUR SCORE

If you answered an item as true and it is listed below as true, then circle that number. If you answered an item as false and it is listed below under false, then circle that number.

True	False
1 2 3 6 8 11 12 13	4 5 7 9 10 14 15 17
16 18 21 22 23 26 28 31	19 20 24 25 27 29 30 34
32 33 36 38 41 42 43 46	35 37 39 40 44 45 47 49
48 51 52 53 56 58 61 62	50 54 55 57 59 60 64 65
63 66 68 71 72 73 76 78	67 69 70 74 75 77 79 80

Total true ....   Total false ....

Total the circles from *both* true and false – this is your total raw score.

Total raw score ....

75

HOW DO YOU COMPARE WITH OTHERS?

To compare yourself with other managers, use the table below. This test is based on international norms of 1,895 managers. Identify your total raw score then read the adjusted category above it. An adjusted category of 5 means that you are in the lowest 5 per cent of managers in coaching relations based on the principles of this test. A score of 75 or more means that you are in the top 25 per cent or so. A higher adjusted category indicates higher coaching relations effectiveness than a lower one.

Adjusted category:	5	15	25	35	45	55	65	75	85	95
Total raw scores:	0–48	49–50	51–52	53–54	55–56	57–58	59–60	61–62	63–64	65–80

PROFILE CHART

Percentile

Management
Coaching
Relations

5 15 25 35 45 55 65 75 85 95

Shade or hatch in your adjusted category from the above section on 'How do you compare with others?' This will be used again for your overall profile in Chapter 15.

WHAT IS BEING MEASURED?

What is being measured by this test is the extent to which you have knowledge of sound methods of coaching members of your team. Most managers are required to coach to some degree as part of their job. It cannot be argued, of course, that all the statements the test claims to be true are in fact true and all the statements the test claims to be false are in fact false. However, it can be said that by and large the statements taken as a whole do reflect what the test measures. You can check the assumption in the test yourself by simply referring to each statement and see whether the test claims it is generally true or generally false. The following statements give an idea of what is believed to be true.

- Coaching often results in a more relaxed and productive work atmosphere.

- It is best if managers know both the subordinate's strengths and weaknesses.

- Managers should coach their subordinates not only on work skills but on human skills as well.

- A prime objective of coaching is to bring out all the reasons for poor performance.

- Subordinates will talk more if the manager really listens to what is said.

- Coaching and appraisal sessions should be held at different times.

- The usefulness of coaching is often increased when the session is held outside the regular work area.

- Productivity will usually increase if a subordinate feels free to talk to the manager in confidence.

- A common cause of low productivity is a person in the wrong job.

- Subordinates can sometimes solve problems themselves if they have the opportunity to talk to others.

- Coaching is essentially a helping relationship.

- Coaching is best when it is informal.

- Coaching is very difficult if the subordinate does not see the need for assistance.

- Coaching is best when the employee decides the way to improve performance.

- Subordinates will talk more if the manager shows interest by appropriate comments.

Some managers are quietly marking time until retirement.

WJR

Each man the architect of his own fate.

Appius Caecus

The manager has the task of creating a true whole that is larger than the sum of its parts, a productive entity that turns out more than the sum of the resources put into it.

Peter F. Drucker

Chapter 6

Self-actualization Inventory

INTRODUCTION

The Self-actualization Inventory measures the degree to which the following needs are unfulfilled; physical, security, relationship, respect, independence and self-actualization. Questions are carefully phrased to avoid putting needs already filled: not 'I enjoy good meals' but rather 'I wish I could enjoy more good meals'. The intensity of the unfulfilled needs is depicted graphically so that a clear needs profile is obtained. Statement items include 'I wish . . .', 'I would like . . .'.

INSTRUCTIONS FOR ANSWERING

Read the first set of three statements (A, B, C) and decide to what extent you agree with each. Assign exactly three points among the three statements. The more points you give a statement the more you agree with it.

Example 1

Suppose you agree with statement A but not at all with any of the others; then you would distribute your points this way:

> A. 3
> B. 0
> C. 0

Example 2

Suppose in another group of statements you agree somewhat with statement B, disagree with statement C, and
do not totally disagree with statement A; then you would
distribute the three points this way:

> A. 1
> B. 2
> C. 0

SELF-ACTUALIZATION INVENTORY

Factor

1.A. I wish that I had more good   A .... (i)
      meals.

    B. I wish that I could buy a   B .... (ii)
      bigger insurance policy.

    C. I wish that I had more   C .... (iii)
      friends.

2.A. I wish I could be more   A .... (ii)
      certain of security in my old
      age.

    B. I wish that I had more   B .... (iii)
      people to talk to.

    C. I wish that I could improve   C .... (vi)
      my knowledge.

3.A. I wish that my job had more   A .... (iv)
      prestige.

  B. I wish that I had a business   B .... (v)
      of my own.

  C. I wish that I could realize my   C .... (vi)
      full potential.

4.A. I wish that my future were   A .... (ii)
      more certain.

  B. I wish more people thought   B .... (iv)
    . highly of me.

  C. I wish that I could achieve   C .... (vi)
      more of my personal goals.

5.A. I wish that I could get more   A .... (i)
      rest.

  B. I would like to be able to   B .... (iii)
      meet more people.

  C. I wish that I were more   C .... (v)
      independent than I am.

6.A. I wish that I had better   A .... (i)
     health.

  B. I wish that I were not alone   B .... (iii)
     as much as I am.

  C. I wish that I could think   C .... (v)
     more independently.

7.A. I wish I knew a safe way out   A .... (ii)
     of my present situation.

  B. I wish that I were more   B .... (iv)
     respected.

  C. I wish that I could develop   C .... (vi)
     myself more than I have.

8.A. I wish that I were in better   A .... (i)
     physical condition.

  B. I wish that I could have   B .... (iv)
     more people to guide and
     direct.

  C. I wish that I could have the   C .... (vi)
     freedom to accomplish what
     I know I can.

9.A. I wish that I could change   A .... (i)
      my weight.

  B. I wish that I worked for   B .... (v)
      myself.

  C. I wish that I had much more   C .... (vi)
      skill in several areas.

10.A. I wish I could plan better for   A .... (ii)
       a safe future.

   B. I wish that I could please   B .... (iii)
       people.

   C. I wish that I got more   C .... (iv)
       recognition for the good
       things I do.

11.A. I wish that I had more   A .... (iii)
       friends who would listen to
       me.

   B. I wish that I questioned   B .... (v)
       more of the things I am told.

   C. I wish that I could learn   C .... (vi)
       more.

12. A. I wish that I had more time to spend relaxing.

    A .... (i)

  B. I wish that I could be more certain of comfort in my old age.

    B .... (ii)

  C. I wish that I took a more prominent part in conversations.

    C .... (iv)

13. A. I wish that I could have more education.

    A .... (ii)

  B. I wish that I knew more people.

    B .... (iii)

  C. I wish that I could think more for myself.

    C .... (v)

14. A. I wish that I could sleep more.

    A .... (i)

  B. I wish that I associated with more community leaders.

    B .... (iv)

  C. I wish that I could have more control over determining what I am to do.

    C .... (v)

15. A. I wish that I knew better ways of gaining attention.

    A .... (iii)

  B. I wish that I got more interest from others.

    B .... (iv)

  C. I wish that I could get some good advice about what I should do.

    C .... (v)

16. A. I wish that I could have more self-confidence.

    A .... (iii)

  B. I wish that I had more close friends.

    B .... (iv)

  C. I wish that I had more comfortable furniture to use.

    C .... (vi)

17. A. I wish that I could make more important decisions.

    A .... (ii)

  B. I wish that I had much more money saved.

    B .... (v)

  C. I wish that I had a more comfortable place to work.

    C .... (vi)

18. A. I wish that I were more determined.   A .... (ii)

    B. I wish that I had more friends among those I work with.   B .... (iv)

    C. I wish that I had a bigger pension coming to me.   C .... (v)

19. A. I wish that I could achieve all of my personal objectives.   A .... (i)

    B. I wish that I did not so readily accept decisions made by others.   B .... (ii)

    C. I wish that I could avoid hurting the feelings of others.   C .... (iv)

20. A. I wish that I could make fewer explanations of why I do things.   A .... (ii)

    B. I wish that travelling were safer.   B .... (v)

    C. I wish that I could go to a doctor more often.   C .... (vi)

21.A. I wish that I could
   continually improve myself.   A .... (i)

   B. I wish other people would do   B .... (ii)
   what I ask them.

   C. I wish that I got more   C .... (vi)
   exercise.

22.A. I wish that I could spend   A .... (i)
   less time and effort on
   unimportant things.

   B. I wish that people did not   B .... (iii)
   disagree with me so much.

   C. I wish that I knew more   C .... (iv)
   people outside work.

23.A. I wish that I could do more   A .... (i)
   worthwhile things.

   B. I wish that I had more   B .... (iii)
   authority.

   C. I wish that I were more   C .... (v)
   cautious.

24. A. I wish that I could develop   A .... (i)
    myself to the fullest extent.

    B. I wish that I could have   B .... (iii)
    more influence on others.

    C. I wish that I played more   C .... (vi)
    sports.

25. A. I wish that I could do every   A .... (i)
    job well.

    B. I wish that I had a more   B .... (iv)
    interesting personality.

    C. I wish that I could do   C .... (vi)
    something about my health.

26. A. I wish that I could take   A .... (i)
    much more pride in the kind
    of work I do.

    B. I wish that I had a more   B .... (v)
    steady and secure job.

    C. I wish that I could do   C .... (vi)
    something about the
    physical conditions at work.

27. A. I wish that I were financially independent.

 A .... (ii)

 B. I wish that I had more pride in myself and in what I do and know.

 B .... (iii)

 C. I wish that I could talk about more topics of interest to others.

 C .... (iv)

28. A. I wish that I could make more of my own decisions.

 A .... (ii)

 B. I wish that I were more important.

 B .... (iii)

 C. I wish I had more guidelines for deciding what to do.

 C .... (v)

HOW TO CALCULATE YOUR SCORE

Add the number of points you allocated to each of these items. The six factor totals should equal 84 when added together.

Factor (i): Physical needs

Unfulfilled needs concerned with filling biological appetites.

Total (i) . . . . .

+

Factor (ii): Security needs

Unfulfilled needs concerned with maintaining safety and security.

Total (ii) . . . . .

+

Factor (iii): Relationship needs

Unfulfilled needs concerned with obtaining love, affection and a feeling of 'belongingness' with others.

Total (iii) . . . . .

+

Factor (iv): Respect needs

Unfulfilled needs concerned with obtaining self-respect, and the esteem of others.

Total (iv) . . . . .

+

Factor (v): Independence needs

Unfulfilled needs concerned with obtaining autonomy.

Total (v) . . . . .

+

Factor (vi): Self-actualization needs

Unfulfilled needs concerned with attaining self-fulfilment.

Total (vi) . . . . .

Grand total = <u>84</u>

HOW DO YOU COMPARE WITH OTHERS?

To compare yourself with 648 other managers, identify your six scores (i) to (vi) in the table below and read above them for the adjusted category, such as Very low (VL). Circle one category in each row.

		Very low VL	Low L	Average ME	High H	Very hi VH
(i)	Physical	0–3	4–5	6–7	8–10	11+
(ii)	Security	0–6	7–9	10–13	14–15	16+
(iii)	Relationship	0–8	9–11	12–13	14–16	17+
(iv)	Respect	0–7	8–9	10–11	12–13	14+
(v)	Independence	0–12	13–14	15–16	17–19	20+
(vi)	Self-actualization	0–23	24–26	27–28	29–32	33+

PROFILE CHART

Self-actualization Inventory	Very low VL	Low L	Average ME	High H	Very high VH
Physical: Unfulfilled needs concerned with filling biological appetites.					
Security: Unfulfilled needs concerned with maintaining safety and security.					
Relationship: Unfulfilled needs concerned with obtaining love, affection and feeling of belongingness with others.					
Respect: Unfulfilled needs concerned with obtaining self-respect and the esteem of others.					
Independence: Unfulfilled needs concerned with obtaining autonomy.					
Self-actualization: Unfulfilled needs concerned with attaining self-fulfilment.					

Shade or hatch in your adjusted category from the above section on 'How do you compare with others?' This will be used again for your overall profile in Chapter 15.

WHAT IS BEING MEASURED?

The six factors being measured are: physical, security, relationship, respect, independence and self-actualization.

Insert your rating
(VL-L-ME-H-VH)

(i) *Physical needs* – unfulfilled needs concerned with filling biological appetites:
'I wish I had more good meals.'
'I wish I could get more rest.'

(ii) *Security needs* – unfulfilled needs concerned with maintaining safety and security:
'I wish I could buy a bigger insurance policy.'
'I wish I could be more certain of security in my old age.'

(iii) *Relationship needs* – unfulfilled needs concerned with obtaining love, affection and a feeling of belongingness with others:
'I wish I had more friends.'
'I would like to be able to meet more people.'

(iv) *Respect needs* – unfulfilled needs concerned with obtaining self-respect and the esteem of others:
'I wish that my job had more prestige.'
'I wish more people thought highly of me.'

(v) *Independence needs* – unfulfilled needs concerned with obtaining autonomy:
'I wish that I had a business of my own.'
'I wish that I worked for myself.'

(vi) *Self-actualization needs* – unfulfilled needs concerned with attaining self-fulfilment:

'I wish that I could realize my full potential.'

'I wish that I could develop myself more than I have.'

This Inventory was developed by W. J. Reddin and K. Rowell © W. J. Reddin, 1991.

He who has a thousand friends,
Has not a friend to spare:
And he who has one enemy,
Shall meet him everywhere.

Omar Khayyam

If we could read the secret history of our enemies, we should find in each man's life sorrow and suffering enough to disarm all hostility.

Longfellow

God Himself, sir, does not propose to judge a man until the end of his days.

Samuel Johnson

Chapter 7

Management Human Relations Test

INTRODUCTION

The Management Human Relations test is an 80-question true/false test of attitudes toward others. Topics covered include relations with superiors, co-workers and subordinates. A high score on this test indicates only a very positive attitude towards others. It does not necessarily follow that this is the best approach by managers in the situation in which they find themselves. A low score, however, does indicate an essentially negative view. The test is jargon-free and is not as much a test of knowledge as of attitude.

INSTRUCTIONS FOR ANSWERING

Read each statement and indicate your answer by circling either T (true) or F (false).

You may find it difficult to make up your mind about some statements. However, in every case circle either T or F.

MANAGEMENT HUMAN RELATIONS TEST

1. Whenever possible each employee's problem should be treated as an individual case on its merits.　　T　F

2. Recognition of work well done will increase employee motivation.　　T　F

---

3. An employee should not have two bosses.   T   F

4. Most union leaders are not really interested in employees.   T   F

5. Most employees have similar backgrounds and should be treated alike.   T   F

6. Different types of work demand quite different approaches to supervision.   T   F

7. Managers should issue all communications in writing.   T   F

8. Employees should be provided with physical comforts whenever possible.   T   F

9. A substantial minority of employees are out to beat the company when they can.   T   F

10. A manager should not take part in departmental social activities.   T   F

11. A good managerial rule is to do to employees as you would have your boss do to you.   T   F

12. Promotions or changes in position should be discussed with the employee well in advance.　T　F

13. Employees will do less work if closely watched and supervised.　T　F

14. There should be no grey areas when interpreting company policy.　T　F

15. Conflict between employees is usually caused by conflicting personalities.　T　F

16. Women clerical workers are at least as effective as male clerical workers.　T　F

17. Employees with less formal education are usually less effective at problem solving.　T　F

18. Whenever possible employees should be allowed to establish their own level of work output.　T　F

19. Humour between employees should be kept at a minimum.　T　F

20. All production plants should require employees to clock in.　T　F

21. Requests for time off are usually reasonable.   T   F

22. Employees work best if they have a say in the way they do their work.   T   F

23. Managers should treat their employees as though the employees were as capable as themselves.   T   F

24. Immediate discipline is usually advisable for insubordination.   T   F

25. A manager should always give advice, if asked, to an employee whose marriage is breaking up.   T   F

26. Managers are not really required for some types of work.   T   F

27. Employees should be told just enough to keep them contented.   T   F

28. Promotions should be based primarily on work effectiveness.   T   F

29. It is often useful to make an example of one employee to so warn others who are breaking the rules.   T   F

30. To maintain control of the depart-
    ment a manager should remain dis-
    tant from the employees.   T   F

31. All employees should be treated first
    as individuals.   T   F

32. Complaints about working condi-
    tions usually reflect an employee's
    hurt feelings about something else.   T   F

33. The more a manager knows about
    an employee the easier it is to main-
    tain discipline.   T   F

34. Most people just work for their pay
    rewards.   T   F

35. Most people prefer being told what to
    do.   T   F

36. Shortening or suspension or eli-
    mination of coffee breaks is seldom
    an effective disciplinary action.   T   F

37. Production and office workers
    should sign in and sign out of each
    working shift.   T   F

38. Employees should always be in-
    formed well in advance of any
    changes that will affect them.   T   F

39. Internal security staff are usually required in most organizations.   T   F

40. Recreation and rest breaks for employees add little to their productivity.   T   F

41. Extra pay should be given for unpleasant work.   T   F

42. A manager should be primarily concerned with the feelings employees have about their work.   T   F

43. Changes are easier to introduce if those affected are involved with the planning of the changes.   T   F

44. A bell signal is a good way to start and stop coffee breaks.   T   F

45. Family sickness should not affect performance.   T   F

46. Most employees could contribute more to departmental productivity.   T   F

47. Personal telephone calls should never be allowed during working hours.   T   F

48. High productivity should be specially rewarded.　　　　　T　F

49. All managers should have an enclosed office.　　　　　T　F

50. Conflict and argument seldom improve things.　　　　　T　F

51. Employees should be encouraged to feel free to discuss any personal problems with their managers.　　　　　T　F

52. Managers often seriously underestimate their employees' true abilities.　　　　　T　F

53. Information on company policy should be widely distributed throughout the organization.　　　　　T　F

54. Union leaders are generally too militant.　　　　　T　F

55. A good way to improve poor employee performance is to let other employees know about it.　　　　　T　F

56. Discipline should be handled by employee and manager alone.　　　　　T　F

57. Managerial pay scales should be kept strictly confidential whenever possible.   T   F

58. Agreement from everyone concerned should at least be sought before a decision is made to introduce a change.   T   F

59. When one or more employees know more than even the good manager, that manager is at a disadvantage.   T   F

60. Letting new employees find out about working procedures the 'hard way' is a good idea.   T   F

61. Obvious discontent among employees is usually the fault of management.   T   F

62. Disciplinary action should be used only as a last resort.   T   F

63. The volume and the amount of talking on the job is often an indicator of interest in the work.   T   F

64. Hints of possible penalties will probably increase employee output.   T   F

65. No eating should take place at a workplace.   T   F

66. Productivity would increase if managers spent more time talking to employees.   T   F

67. The personnel department should handle most human relations type problems.   T   F

68. There should be no fixed penalty for lateness.   T   F

69. Most work problems need a manager to solve them.   T   F

70. Union leaders contribute little to productivity.   T   F

71. An employee newspaper will usually increase productivity.   T   F

72. So-called illegal work stoppages are sometimes justified.   T   F

73. Employees should feel free to contribute to layout in every way they think they can.   T   F

74. Even five minutes of lateness should be penalized.   T   F

75. Pay is almost always a good way to motivate.   T   F

76. Company personnel policy should first consider the wellbeing of the employee.   T   F

77. Most employees cannot find work personally satisfying in itself.   T   F

78. Employees should be given the benefit of the doubt when infractions of rules occur.   T   F

79. Employee loyalty to the company can easily be achieved.   T   F

80. A manager should ignore the 'grapevine'.   T   F

HOW TO CALCULATE YOUR SCORE

If you answered an item as true and it is listed below as true, then circle that number. If you answered an item as false and it is listed below under false, then circle that number.

True	False
1 2 3 6 8 11 12 13	4 5 7 9 10 14 15 17
16 18 21 22 23 26 28 31	19 20 24 25 27 29 30 34
32 33 36 38 41 42 43 46	35 37 39 40 44 45 47 49
48 51 52 53 56 58 61 62	50 54 55 57 59 60 64 65
63 66 68 71 72 73 76 78	67 69 70 74 75 77 79 80

Total true ....   Total false ....

Total the circles from *both* true and false – this is your total raw score.

Total raw score ....

HOW DO YOU COMPARE WITH OTHERS?

To compare yourself with other managers, use the table below. This test is based on international norms of 1,895 managers. Identify your total raw score then read the adjusted category above it. An adjusted category of 5 means that you are in the lowest 5 per cent of managers in human relations based on the principles of this test. A score of 75 or more means that you are in the top 25 per cent or so. A higher adjusted category indicates higher human relations effectiveness than a lower one.

Adjusted category:	5	15	25	35	45	55	65	75	85	95
Total raw scores:	0–38	39–41	42–44	45–46	47–48	49–52	53–54	55–56	57–60	61–8(

PROFILE CHART

Percentile

Management Human Relations	5	15	25	35	45	55	65	75	85	95

Shade or hatch in your adjusted category from the above section on 'How do you compare with others?' This will be used again for your overall profile in Chapter 15.

WHAT IS BEING MEASURED?

What is being measured by this test is your attitude to others. It may or may not fit you or your situation at the moment but it does seem to fit many others. It cannot be argued, of course, that all the statements the test claims to be true are in fact true and all the statements the test claims to be false are in fact false. However, it can be said that by and large the statements taken as a whole do reflect what the test measures. You can check the assumption in the test yourself by simply referring to each statement and see whether the test claims it is generally true or generally false. The following statements give an idea of what is believed to be false.

- Managers should issue all communications in writing.

- A substantial minority of employees are out to beat the company when they can.

- A manager should not take part in departmental social activities.

- Conflict between employees is usually caused by conflicting personalities.

- A manager should ignore the 'grapevine'.

- Employees with less formal education are usually less effective at problem solving.

- Humour between employees should be kept at a minimum.

- All production plants should require employees to clock in.

- Promotions should be based primarily on work effectiveness.

- Production and office employees should sign in and sign out of each working shift.

- The personnel department should handle most human relations type problems.

This Test was developed by W. J. Reddin and E. K. Stewart © W. J. Reddin, 1991.

How can we avoid the two extremes; too great bossism in giving orders, and practically no orders given? . . . My solution is to depersonalize the giving of orders, to unite all concerned in a study of the situation, to discover the law of the situation and obey that.

Mary Parker Follett

Committee: a group that keeps minutes but squanders hours.

Unknown

Chapter 8

Management Communication Relations Test

INTRODUCTION

The Management Communication Relations test is an 80-question true/false test of knowledge of sound communication methods. Topics covered include communication with subordinates, co-workers and superiors; orders; introduction of change; verbal and non-verbal communication. The test is jargon-free and emphasizes principles and common sense rather than theory.

INSTRUCTIONS FOR ANSWERING

Read each statement and indicate your answer by circling either T (true) or F (false).

You may find it difficult to make up your mind about some statements. However, in every case circle either T or F.

MANAGEMENT COMMUNICATION RELATIONS TEST

1. Employees who are well informed will work more effectively.   T   F

2. Recognition of work well done will increase employee motivation.   T   F

---

3. Employees should be told in advance of those changes which will affect them.   T   F

4. Company policy need not be communicated below the management level.   T   F

5. Employees should be discouraged from suggesting alternate ways of doing work.   T   F

6. A manager's influence usually increases when seeking advice from employees.   T   F

7. All important communication is either spoken or written.   T   F

8. If they were listened to, most employees could contribute more to productivity.   T   F

9. A manager should write as many communications as possible.   T   F

10. For effective communication, meeting-rooms should be arranged in classroom fashion.   T   F

11. Minutes recorded at work meetings could be very useful if they contained only the decisions made and not the discussion. T F

12. Different situations demand quite different styles. T F

13. Complaints about working conditions sometimes really reflect an employee's hurt feelings. T F

14. The more technically skilled a manager is the better the understanding by employees. T F

15. As much as possible of a manager's communication to the superior should be in writing. T F

16. Managers should consider employee complaints from the employee's point of view. T F

17. Files of inter-departmental memos should be maintained to establish responsibility for decisions made. T F

18. Productivity would probably increase if coffee breaks were used as meeting opportunities for managers and their superiors. T F

19. Evaluation of employees' perform-
    ance should always be in writing.   T   F

20. Employees should be told just
    enough to keep them content.   T   F

21. Talking to someone in person is
    usually more effective than using the
    telephone.   T   F

22. The volume of talking in a workplace
    can indicate enthusiasm.   T   F

23. Quiet employees should be encour-
    aged to speak at problem-solving
    meetings even though their con-
    tribution may slow down the
    meeting.   T   F

24. Recreation and rest breaks for em-
    ployees add little to productivity.   T   F

25. In order to be understood a manager
    must be good at spelling.   T   F

26. Poor education is seldom a cause of
    communication breakdown.   T   F

27. Disagreement should be avoided at
    meetings.   T   F

28. A manager can check if an employee is listening by watching the employee's face.   T   F

29. More effective communication usually results if the manager does not spare the employees' feelings.   T   F

30. Effectiveness of communication will be increased if the manager is 'one of the boys or girls'.   T   F

31. A manager must show a willingness to see different points of view.   T   F

32. The best manager listens more than talks.   T   F

33. Effective communication only takes place when the listener fully understands the message.   T   F

34. Sarcasm should be used occasionally with specific employees to get them to change.   T   F

35. Employees usually work better when they do not hear too much about the quality of their performance.   T   F

36. Repeating what someone else has said is a good way to check to see if you understood the message.   T   F

37. In conversation, a silence after a point has been made can usually be taken to mean agreement.   T F

38. People often don't listen too well to things they don't agree with.   T F

39. Managers with large vocabularies are more likely to communicate better.   T F

40. A manager should report problems to the superior rather than suggest solutions.   T F

41. Counselling and communication are central to good management.   T F

42. The person who sits at the head of the conference table would often like to be chairperson.   T F

43. Participation need not involve acceptance by managers of the employee's suggestions.   T F

44. Because tone of voice can change the meaning of words, messages should be written whenever possible.   T F

45. Talking between employees will usually result in lower productivity.   T F

46. If managers cannot size up situations, their communication will be poor.　　　　　　　　　　T　F

47. Good listeners often doodle while someone is talking to them.　　　　　T　F

48. Employees work better if they are kept fully informed.　　　　　　　T　F

49. If employees shift their feet or eyes while listening, it is usually unimportant and should not concern the manager.　　　　　　　　　　T　F

50. A rumour at work known to be false is not worth listening to.　　　　　　T　F

51. Some of the notice boards announcing company decisions should be placed in non-work areas of the plant.　　　　　　　　　　　T　F

52. Chairpeople often slow down meetings.　　　　　　　　　　　　T　F

53. Moving back one's chair at a meeting probably indicates disinterest.　　　T　F

54. Employees will usually tell a manager when they do not understand.　　T　F

55. The employee has the primary responsibility for listening to and understanding the manager's communication.　　　　T　F

56. Many distortions occur when messages are passed by word of mouth from one person to another.　　　　T　F

57. Most meetings between the manager and the superior should be formal and regularly scheduled.　　　　T　F

58. As much information as possible should be given in advance of a change.　　　　T　F

59. Changes in company policy which are likely to be controversial should simply be announced with no discussion.　　　　T　F

60. Explaining communication principles will almost always improve communication.　　　　T　F

61. Communication usually breaks down when the manager does not take employees' feelings into account.　　　　T　F

62. Questioning is a good method to use when checking whether messages are understood.　　　　T　F

63. The use of some humour will usually improve communication. T F

64. Notice boards should be used exclusively for management announcements. T F

65. All problem-solving meetings should have a secretary and a formal chairperson. T F

66. Productivity would increase if managers spent more time talking to their employees. T F

67. All departmental decisions should be made by the manager. T F

68. Watching a speaker's face increases communication. T F

69. Discussion of a decision after it is made usually leads directly to lower productivity. T F

70. When company policy is clearly understood by the manager it can usually be assumed that it will be understood by the employees. T F

71. Communication is more effective when employees feel free to discuss any subject with their manager. T F

72. A condition of too much communication can occur.   T   F

73. Supplying large amounts of advance
information concerning a change
will reduce resistance to it.   T   F

74. Everyone understands what participative management means.   T   F

75. Notices should be placed near the
manager's office and this will make
it more likely they will be read.   T   F

76. Face-to-face announcements are
almost always better than the written word.   T   F

77. Employees with less formal education are usually less effective at communication.   T   F

78. Hints of disciplinary action for a
violation will decrease the effectiveness of a manager's order.   T   F

79. Most employees have similar backgrounds and should be treated alike.   T   F

80. When communicating, the manager's sole concern should be with the
facts.   T   F

HOW TO CALCULATE YOUR SCORE

If you answered an item as true and it is listed below as true, then circle that number. If you answered an item as false and it is listed below under false, then circle that number.

True	False
1 2 3 6 8 11 12 13	4 5 7 9 10 14 15 17
16 18 21 22 23 26 28 31	19 20 24 25 27 29 30 34
32 33 36 38 41 42 43 46	35 37 39 40 44 45 47 49
48 51 52 53 56 58 61 62	50 54 55 57 59 60 64 65
63 66 68 71 72 73 76 78	67 69 70 74 75 77 79 80

Total true ....   Total false ....

Total the circles from *both* true and false – this is your total raw score.

Total Raw Score ....

HOW DO YOU COMPARE WITH OTHERS?

To compare yourself with other managers, use the table below. This test is based on international norms of 1,895 managers. Identify your total raw score then read the adjusted category above it. An adjusted category of 5 means that you are in the lowest 5 per cent of managers in communication relations based on the principles of this test. A score of 75 or more means that you are in the top 25 per cent or so. A higher adjusted category indicates higher communication relations effectiveness than a lower one.

Adjusted category:	5	15	25	35	45	55	65	75	85	95
Total raw scores:	0–44	45–46	47–50	51–52	53–54	55–56	57–58	59–60	61–64	65–80

PROFILE CHART

Percentile

Management	5	15	25	35	45	55	65	75	85	95
Communica-tion Relations										

Shade or hatch in your adjusted category from the above section on 'How do you compare with others?' This will be used again for your overall profile in Chapter 15.

WHAT IS BEING MEASURED?

What is being measured by this test is the extent to which you have knowledge of sound methods of communication with members of your team. It cannot be argued, of course, that all the statements the test claims to be true are in fact true and all the statements the test claims to be false are in fact false. However, it can be said that by and large the statements taken as a whole do reflect what the test measures. You can check the assumption in the test yourself by simply referring to each statement and see whether the test claims it is generally true or generally false. The following statements give an idea of what is believed to be true.

- Employees who are well informed will work more effectively.

- A manager's influence usually increases when seeking advice from employees.

- Complaints about working conditions sometimes really reflect an employee's hurt feelings.

- Managers should consider employee complaints from the employee's point of view.

- The volume of talking in a workplace can indicate enthusiasm.

- The best manager listens more than talks.

- People don't often listen well to things they don't agree with.

- If managers cannot size up situations, their communication will be poor.

This Test was developed by W. J. Reddin, E. K. Stewart and K. J. Rowell

Man's capacities have never been measured; nor are we to judge of what he can do by any precedents, so little has been tried.

H. D. Thoreau

Motivation is not what you do to people, it is what you allow them to do to themselves.

WJR

Chapter 9

XYZ Inventory

INTRODUCTION

This inventory is to inform you about your underlying managerial assumptions in terms of the average person being seen as a beast (X), a self-actualizing being (Y), or a rational being (Z).

Assumptions (X) and (Y) are taken directly from McGregor, D. V. *The Human Side of Enterprise*, McGraw Hill, New York, 1960.

INSTRUCTIONS FOR ANSWERING

Read the first set of two statements (1a and 1b) and decide to what extent you agree with each. Assign exactly three points between the two statements. The more points you give to a statement the more you agree with it.

Example 1
Supposing that you agree fully with statement 1a and disagree with statement 1b, you would distribute your points in this way:

  3 – Statement 1a
  0 – Statement 1b

Example 2
Supposing that you agree with statement 1b and do not totally disagree with statement 1a, you would distribute the points this way:

  1 – Statement 1a
  2 – Statement 1b

XYZ INVENTORY

1a People like to compete with each other.

1b People prefer co-operation above all else.

2a To get a person to perform most effectively it is best to offer a reward.

2c The best way to understand people is to see them as reasoning human beings.

3b The majority of people trust each other.

3c Clear explanations usually lead to higher levels of co-operation.

4a People will work harder when competing with one another.

4b People are best understood when studied as social beings.

5a The main reason most people work is for money.

5c The only function of discipline is to prevent recurrence.

6b The true function of government is to aid society.

6c People always prefer to reason with other people.

7a Most successful people compete well.

7b Teamwork usually produces good results.

8a People will usually do a better job if offered more money.

8c People usually do what they think they should.

9b People respond more readily to encouragement than to punishment.

9c Successful people know how and when to depend on others.

10a The basic function of government is to control society.

10b Mankind's future is promising.

11a Most successful leaders have to learn that to divide and rule is sometimes a necessary management technique.

11c The best way to get someone to do a job well is to explain clearly what is involved.

12b Work is as natural as play or rest.

12c Governments should influence man by reason.

13a People will sometimes interfere with what other people want to do just to gain an advantage for themselves.

13b People enjoy working and living with other people.

14a There is no particular reason to be optimistic about mankind's future.

14c Individual behaviour depends primarily on the forces in the situation.

15b Everyone could like everyone else.

15c Followers are best controlled when the situation as they see it is understood.

16a Teamwork often results in compromise.

16b A person should be willing to die to save friends.

17a When all things are considered man does at least as much harm as good.

17c The best method of leadership is to size up the situation first and then to take action.

18b Do only to other people what you would have them do to you.

18c The future of mankind is what mankind wants it to be.

19a A person's life is a continual attempt to satisfy personal needs.

19b When people co-operate with one another they usually produce more.

20a Most people look out for themselves first.
20c People are very adaptable.

21b Most successful people co-operate well with others.

21c The best way to motivate people is to let them know how they are doing.

22c Some competition is healthy but too much of it results in unnecessary conflict.

22b People's most useful resources are the friends who know them well.

23c A person fights only when peace is not wanted.

23a A person is essentially a naked ape.

24b When people have followers it is best to treat them as friends.

24a Discipline is a good way to correct violations and improve performance.

25c Individuals decide their own lives.

25b People work best with friends.

26c Change tends to stabilize rather than to upset things.

26a Warfare is a natural human condition.

27b People will harm others only when forced to.

27c True teamwork is almost impossible to achieve.

28c Lack of knowledge is the main thing holding mankind back.

28b One's life is best seen as a constant attempt to improve oneself and one's society.

29c Mankind's greatest ability is to reason.

29a Leaders tend to serve their own needs first.

30b People will protect friends before saving themselves.

30a Mankind has not yet earned itself a peaceful life.

31c Life would be better if people made more use of their brains.

31b True teamwork is worth working for and, with effort, easy to achieve.

32c People find the human condition painful because of their intelligence.

32a People are by nature destructive.

33b People have more strengths than weaknesses if only they are motivated to use them.

33a Pollution is caused by mankind's selfishness.

34c People have the potential ability to be effective in almost any situation.

34b Leaders serve their followers' needs first.

35c True teamwork is worthwhile but difficult to achieve.

35a People have more weaknesses than strengths.

36b Mankind, by its inherent nature, is constructive.

36a There is no real evidence that we can control our natural instincts.

37c The best way to understand people is to see them as reasoning human beings.

37b Co-operation is natural to people.

38c People usually do what they think they should.

38a Bargaining is as natural to people as eating and sleeping.

39a People usually get what they deserve.

39b Mankind does not need to be governed by laws.

40c The future of mankind is what mankind wants it to be.

40b Performance is not increased by discipline.

41c People fight only when they do not want peace.

41a Mankind lives in fear of pain and suffering.

42b Mankind does more good than harm.

42a To really understand mankind we should study animal behaviour.

HOW TO CALCULATE YOUR SCORE

Add all the points you assigned to each type of statement (a, b and c), entering each total in the space provided on the right hand side of each page. (The total of a plus b plus c should be 126.)

Factor 1 Theory 'X': Assumptions about the nature of man
Man is basically a beast who is best controlled by civilization; he is inherently evil, is driven by his biological impulses; his basic interactional mode is competition.

The assumptions held are best reflected by the following kinds of thoughts:

'People like to compete with each other'
'To get a person to perform most effectively it is best to offer a reward'
'The main reason most people work is for money'
'The basic function of government is to control society'

Total a ....

Factor 2 Theory 'Y': Assumptions about the nature of man

Man is basically a self-actualizing person who works best with few controls; he is inherently good, is driven by his humanism; his basic interactional mode is co-operation.

The assumptions held are best reflected by the following kinds of thoughts:

'People prefer co-operation above all else'
'The majority of people trust each other'
'The true function of government is to aid society'
'Teamwork usually produces good results'

Total b ....

Factor 3 Theory 'Z': Assumptions about the nature of man

Man is basically a rational being open to and controlled by reason; he is inherently neither good nor evil but open to both, is driven by his intellect; his basic interactional mode is independence.

The assumptions held are best reflected by the following kinds of thoughts:

'The best way to understand people is to see them as reasoning human beings'
'Clear explanations usually lead to higher levels of co-operation'
'People usually do what they think they should'
'The best way to get someone to do a job well is to explain clearly what is involved'

Total c ....

Total raw scores (a + b + c) = 126

Do not pay any attention to the relative size of these total raw scores. They must be converted if you are to compare yourself with other managers.

HOW DO YOU COMPARE WITH OTHERS?

To compare yourself with 648 other managers, identify your three raw scores (a, b and c) in the table below and read above them for the adjusted categories.

Scale	Very low VL	Low L	Average ME	High H	Very high VH
a	Up to 10	11–24	25–35	36–49	50+
b	Up to 9	10–16	17–25	26–47	48+
c	Up to 10	11–24	25–35	36–49	50+

For instance, if you scored 10 or below on scale a, it means you are very low compared with other managers on your assumptions that man is basically a beast.

PROFILE CHART

	Very low VL	Low L	Aver- age ME	High H	Very high VH
XYZ Inventory a					
b					
c					

Shade or hatch in your adjusted category from the above section on 'How do you compare with others?' This will be used again for your overall profile in Chapter 15.

This Inventory was developed by W. J. Reddin and B. Sullivan © W. J. Reddin, 1991.

Life is not long, and too much of it must not pass in idle deliberation how it shall be spent.

Samuel Johnson

A great deal of energy is spent on work which is completely unnecessary.

G. I. Guardjieff

Improved time management provides great potential for increased effectiveness.

WJR

Chapter 10

Time Usage Diary

INSTRUCTIONS

This Time Usage Diary has six pages of the same design. The Diary is used by a manager or a secretary to record the manager's activity over a one-week period.

These activities are analyzed by the manager using one or more of the sets of categories below, or other categories. By this analysis the manager obtains a clear picture of how time is spent. Each category forms a set within which time can be fully allocated.

Information time distribution
- (IR) Retrieval-storage (reading)
- (IE) Expansion (writing/creative work/thinking)
- (ID) Distribution (talking/memos/letters)

Hierarchal time distribution (excludes being alone)
- (HS) With superior
- (HC) With co-workers
- (HU) With subordinates

Interaction time distribution
- (NO) Alone (includes with secretary)
- (N1) With one person
- (N2) With more than one person

Location time distribution
- (LI)   In own office
- (LB)   Outside office/in building
- (LO)   Outside building

Employee time distribution
- (EA)   Alone
- (EE)   With company employees
- (EN)   With non-employees

Paperwork time distribution
- (PG)   Generating paperwork
- (PD)   Dealing with company paperwork
- (PN)   Not paperwork

Period time distribution
Matters whose most important effect is:
- (TM)   Within one month
- (TY)   Within one year
- (TO)   Over one year

Skill time distribution
Could be done by:
- (SO)   Others easily
- (ST)   Others with short training
- (SV)   Others only with very long training

Delegation time distribution
- (DM) Must be done by me
- (DO) Could be done by others
- (DS) Should be done by others

Time Usage Diary

DAY
MONTH
YEAR

HOUR	ACTIVITY	TIME	ANALYSIS	TIME
7				
8				
9				
10				
11				
12				
1				
2				
3				
4				
5				
6				
EVEN-ING				
	TOTAL TIME		**TOTAL TIME**	

Tests for the Output-oriented Manager

DAY
MONTH
YEAR

HOUR	ACTIVITY	TIME	ANALYSIS	TIME
7				
8				
9				
10				
11				
12				
1				
2				
3				
4				
5				
6				
EVEN-ING				
	TOTAL TIME		**TOTAL TIME**	

Time Usage Diary

DAY
MONTH
YEAR

HOUR	ACTIVITY	TIME	ANALYSIS	TIME
7				
8				
9				
10				
11				
12				
1				
2				
3				
4				
5				
6				
EVEN-ING				
	TOTAL TIME		**TOTAL TIME**	

151

DAY
MONTH
YEAR

HOUR	ACTIVITY	TIME	ANALYSIS	TIME
7				
8				
9				
10				
11				
12				
1				
2				
3				
4				
5				
6				
EVEN-ING				
	TOTAL TIME		**TOTAL TIME**	

Time Usage Diary

DAY
MONTH
YEAR

HOUR	ACTIVITY	TIME	ANALYSIS	TIME
7				
8				
9				
10				
11				
12				
1				
2				
3				
4				
5				
6				
EVEN-ING				
	TOTAL TIME		**TOTAL TIME**	

DAY
MONTH
YEAR

HOUR	ACTIVITY	TIME	ANALYSIS	TIME
7				
8				
9				
10				
11				
12				
1				
2				
3				
4				
5				
6				
EVEN-ING				
	TOTAL TIME		**TOTAL TIME**	

PROFILE CHART

Based on this one-week period, make a self-assessment of your effective use of time by completing the profile chart below.

	Very low VL	Low L	Aver- age ME	High H	Very high VH
Time Usage Diary					

Shade or hatch in your category. This will be used again for your overall profile in Chapter 15.

List below why you gave yourself the rating you did.

1.

2.

3.

4.

5.

This Indicator was developed by W. J. Reddin
© W. J. Reddin, 1991.

Some managers have no philosophy and their style is essentially that of the bland leading the bland.

WJR

Every man is in certain respects
- *a) like all other men*
- *b) like some other man*
- *c) like no other man.*

Clyde Kluckhorn and Henry A. Murray

The beginning of administrative wisdom is the awareness that there is no one optimum type of management system.

Tom Burns

Chapter 11

Basic Style Indicator Test

INTRODUCTION

The objective of this chapter is to get you to think about your current basic style of management and also about other basic styles available. You will then be able to think in detail about applying the correct basic style based on your analysis of your situation in order to increase effectiveness.

THE THEORY BEHIND THE TEST

Two orientations

As with the analysis of situations, there has been a great deal of research by many investigators into managerial style. A point on which there is virtual agreement is that it is useful to think of managerial behaviour as having two orientations: task orientation and relationships orientation (see Figure 11.1).

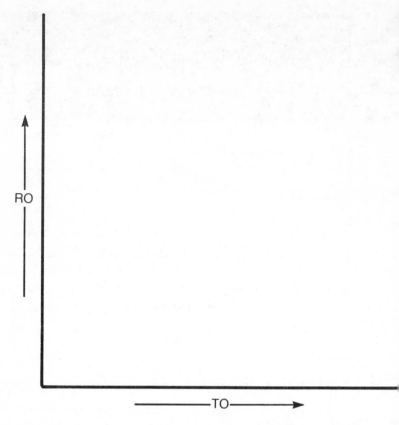

Figure 11.1. Task and relationships orientations

The titles pretty well explain the terms themselves; however, the definitions are as follows:

- *Task orientation (TO)*: The extent to which managers direct their efforts; characterized by initiating, organizing and directing.

- *Relationships orientation (RO)*: The extent to which a manager has personal job relationships; characterized by listening, trusting and encouraging.

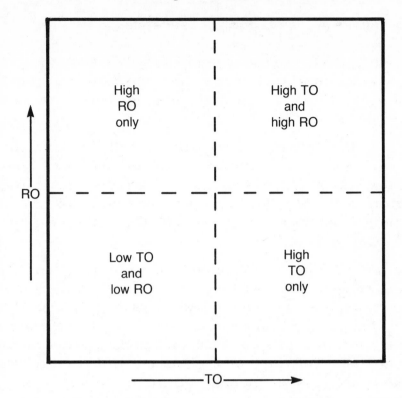

Figure 11.2. Four types of behaviour

FOUR BASIC STYLES

These two important dimensions of managerial behaviour are independent of each other. A manager can be
high on one and low on the other, high on both or low on
both. This leads to the kind of diagram shown in Figure
11.2. Because these two dimensions are independent one
can derive four basic styles which mirror the four basic
situational demands. These four basic styles represent
some managers who are separated from both task and
relationships in their situations, some who are mainly
concerned with relationships, some who are mainly dedicated to the job, and finally others who have a major
interest in integrating relationships and task.

Differences across the four basic styles

Obviously the four basic styles are very different – the test gives a clear indication of this. It is worth studying these differences in detail now and thinking about your own natural basic style.

Look at the first two of the 23 items of the test. The interactional mode of the separated manager is correcting deviations. The related manager accepts others. The dedicated manager tends to dominate and direct. The integrated manager wants to join with others in the service of work.

The preferred mode of communication of the separated manager is written, as this involves less relationships orientation and can involve lower task orientation. The related manager obviously prefers to talk. The dedicated manager wants to give vocal directions as this helps domination. The integrated manager, rather obviously, prefers meetings. All managers bring to situations their natural propensities; however, a professional manager is concerned primarily with serving what the situation demands, not serving self.

INSTRUCTIONS

Read over each of the 23 items of the test. As you read each line, spread ten points in the boxes provided for each line. For example:

Interactional mode

Correcting	3
Accepting	3
Dominating	0
Joining	4

Total 10

Mode of communication

Written	7
Conversation	0
Vocal directions	0
Meetings	3

Total 10

When you have completed this, add up the total you have for each column. This grand total will be 230.

BASIC STYLE INDICATOR TEST

	Separated	Related	Dedicated	Integrated		
1. Interactional mode	Correcting	Accepting	Dominating	Joining	=	10
2. Mode of communication	Written	Conversation	Vocal directions	Meetings	=	10
3. Direction of communication	Little in any direction	Upwards from subordinates	Downwards to subordinates	Two-way	=	10
4. Time perspective	Post	Unconcerned	Immediate	Future	=	10
5. Identifies with	Organization	Subordinates	Superior and technology	Co-workers	=	10
6. Systems emphasis	Maintains procedural system	Supports social system	Follows technological system	Integrates socio-technical system	=	10
7. Judges subordinates on	Who follows the rules?	Who understands people?	Who produces?	Who wants to join the team?	=	10
8. Judges superior on	Brains	Warmth	Power	Teamwork	=	10
9. Committee activity	Clarifying, guiding, channelling	Supporting, harmonizing, coaching	Initiating, evaluating, directing	Setting standards, testing, motivating	=	10
10. Work suited for	Administration, accounting, statistics, design	Managing professionals, training, coordinating	Production, sales management	Supervizing interacting managers	=	10
11. Work	Non-routine	Low personal	Low power	High routine	=	10

13. Reaction to error	More controls	Pass over	Punish	Learn from	= 10
14. Reaction to conflict	Avoids	Smothers	Suppresses	Utilize	= 10
15. Reaction to stress	Withdraws and quotes rules	Becomes dependent and depressed	Dominates and exploits	Avoids making decisions	= 10
16. Positive source of control	Logic	Praise	Rewards	Ideals	= 10
17. Negative source of control	Argument	Rejection	Punishment	Compromise	= 10
18. Characteristic problem of subordinates	Lack of recognition	Lack of direction	Lack of information	Lack of independence	= 10
19. Punishment used	Loss of authority	Loss of interest by manager	Loss of position	Loss of self-respect by subordinates	= 10
20. Undervalues	Need for innovation	Needs of organization and of technology	Subordinates' expectations	Need for independent action	= 10
21. Main weakness	Slave to the rules	Sentimentality	Fights unnecessarily	Uses participation inappropriately	= 10
22. Fears about self	Emotionality, softness and dependence	Rejection by others	Loss of power	Uninvolvement	= 10
23. Fears about others	System deviation irrationality	Conflict	Production	Dissatisfaction	= 10
Totals					= 230

THE FOUR STYLES OF MANAGER

The separated style of manager

Separated managerial behaviour is characterized by both low task and low relationships orientation, i.e. behaviour literally separated from both people and task. The separated manager is really oriented to nothing changing, only to system maintenance.

Indicators

- Cautious/careful/conservative
- Prefers paperwork
- Looks for established principles
- Accurate/precise/correct
- Steady/deliberate/patient
- Calm/modest/discreet.

The related style of manager

Related managerial behaviour is characterized by low task orientation and high relationships orientation. It is called related because of its emphasis on relationships with people. The related manager tends to be accepting and friendly and to create a secure atmosphere for others to work in.

Indicators

- People come first
- Emphasizes personal development
- Informal/quiet/unnoticed
- Long conversations
- Sympathetic/accepting/friendly
- Creates secure atmosphere.

The dedicated style of manager

Managerial behaviour characterized by high task orienta
tion but low relationships orientation is designated ded
cated because of its emphasis on task completion. Th
dedicated manager tends to be hardworking, aggressiv
and independent.

Indicators

- Determined/aggressive/confident
- Busy/driving/initiating
- Sets individual tasks and standards
- Self-reliant/independent/ambitious
- Uses rewards, punishments, controls
- Tasks come first.

The integrated style of manager

Managerial behaviour characterized by both high task and high relationships orientation is called integrated because it combines both orientations. The integrated manager prefers shared objectives – teamwork.

Indicators

- Derives authority from aims and ideals

- Integrates individual with organization

- Wants participation

- Prefers shared objectives

- Interested in motivational techniques

- Prefers teamwork.

PROFILE CHART

Transfer your raw scores for each column to the profile chart below.

Basic Style Indicator Test

	Raw Score	0–40	41–80	81–120	121–160	161+
Sep						
Rel						
Ded						
Int						

= **230**

Shade or hatch in your raw scores in the profile chart for each of the four basic styles. This will be used again for your overall profile in Chapter 15.

This Test was designed by W. J. Reddin
© W. J. Reddin, 1991.

This Test is copyright in all countries and it is illegal to photocopy it. Copies may be obtained from the addresses given in Chapter 20.

If you don't know where you are going, any road will get you there.

The Koran

Some managers let the in-basket define the nature of their contribution and the clock its limit.

WJR

Choose a job you love, and you will never have to work a day in your life.

Confucius

Chapter 12

Managerial Task Inventory

3-D THEORY

Recent advances in Management Style theory have identified eight distinct approaches to any management situation. No single approach is always best, or even possible. Effectiveness depends on the degree to which the approach fits the needs of the situation in which it is used.

Management Task Inventory

This Inventory allows a manager to identify the particular styles that were found useful or necessary in the everyday exercise of the managerial function. The manager may also use it to identify the styles of others, such as members of a management team, or of subordinates. The Inventory is composed of eight element scales, each having eight statements. The eight scales each refer to some element of the managerial task, and are under the headings of Creativity, Data collection, Setting objectives, Planning, Introducing change, Implementation, Productivity, and Evaluation.

Each of the eight statements of each scale refers to a different way of dealing with the particular element in question. Thus under the element scale 'Creativity' we find, for example,

- (S) I believe the value of creativity, change and innovation is often overemphasized.
- (T) I think that many new ideas lead to unnecessary disagreement and friction.

INSTRUCTIONS

To identify your own style:

1. Look at the eight statements of the first element scale 'Creativity'.

2. Distribute ten points over not more than four statements to indicate the degree to which the statements reflect your own management style. You may allocate all ten points to one statement, or five to each of two, or in any other way. Do not assign points to more than four statements. (For your convenience this instruction has been repeated below each of the eight element scales.)

3. Continue now to the second element scale and so on through all eight scales. When you have finished you will have ten points distributed over each scale.

4. Use the Inventory Summary on page 181 to summarize your distribution of points. Then add the points allocated to each statement and record the total in the box next to the style letters on the left. These will total 80.

1.   CREATIVITY

S   I believe the value of creativity, change and innovation is often overemphasized.

     ....

T   I think that many new ideas lead to unnecessary disagreement and friction.

     ....

U   I think new ideas from below are often less useful than those from above.

     ....

V   I sometimes encourage new ideas but do not always follow up on too many of them.

     ....

W   I believe that formal meetings are a perfectly sound way to produce ideas.

     ....

X   I seek out new and good ideas and motivate others to be as creative as possible.

     ....

Y   I both develop and propose many new ideas.

     ....

Z   I am constantly on the watch for new, useful and productive ideas from any source and develop many ideas myself.

     ....

Distribute ten points over not more than four statements to indicate the degree to which the statements reflect your own management style. You may allocate all ten points to one statement, or five to each of two, or in any other way. Do not assign points to more than four statements.

2. DATA COLLECTION

T   I am sometimes reluctant to ask for or to challenge information if it might hurt someone's feelings.

....

U   I am skilled at 'shooting down' those who try to provide me with information.

....

V   I am usually receptive to information but do not always utilize what I am given.

....

W   I am particularly receptive to information that comes through the regular company channels.

....

X   I successfully encourage others to obtain information and pay attention to what they have to say.

....

Y   I obtain as much information as possible before making a decision. I value advice from superiors and experts more than from subordinates.

....

Z   I successfully tap every source of information available to me.

....

S   I do not search out enough information to do a good job.

....

Distribute ten points over not more than four statements to indicate the degree to which the statements reflect your own management style. You may allocate all ten points to one statement, or five to each of two, or in any other way. Do not assign points to more than four statements.

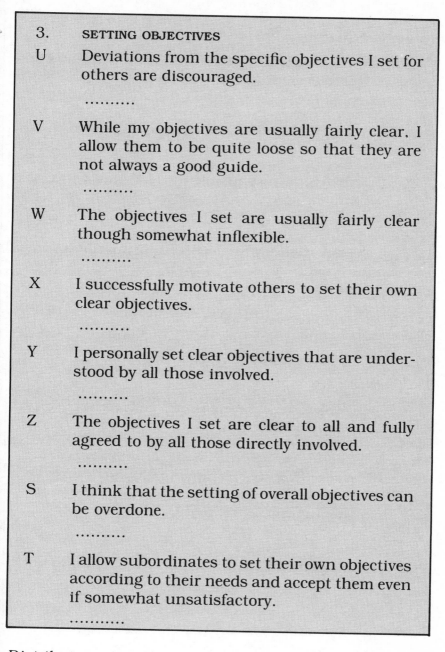

3. **SETTING OBJECTIVES**

U   Deviations from the specific objectives I set for others are discouraged.

....

V   While my objectives are usually fairly clear, I allow them to be quite loose so that they are not always a good guide.

....

W   The objectives I set are usually fairly clear though somewhat inflexible.

....

X   I successfully motivate others to set their own clear objectives.

....

Y   I personally set clear objectives that are understood by all those involved.

....

Z   The objectives I set are clear to all and fully agreed to by all those directly involved.

....

S   I think that the setting of overall objectives can be overdone.

....

T   I allow subordinates to set their own objectives according to their needs and accept them even if somewhat unsatisfactory.

....

Distribute ten points over not more than four statements to indicate the degree to which the statements reflect your own management style. You may allocate all ten points to one statement, or five to each of two, or in any other way. Do not assign points to more than four statements.

4.	**PLANNING**
V	I make an effort at planning but the plans do not always work out.
	....
W	I plan with a fine attention to detail.
	....
X	When I am responsible for planning I involve many others.
	....
Y	I plan well and concentrate primarily on my own good ideas and assign individual responsibilities.
	....
Z	When I am involved the plans made represent the best thinking of all concerned.
	....
S	I think that planning is not really as important as some people think.
	....
T	I prefer to let each individual make their own plans as long as they do not interfere with the plans of others.
	....
U	I see planning as a one-person job and do not usually involve others or their ideas.
	....

Distribute ten points over not more than four statements to indicate the degree to which the statements reflect your own management style. You may allocate all ten points to one statement, or five to each of two, or in any other way. Do not assign points to more than four statements.

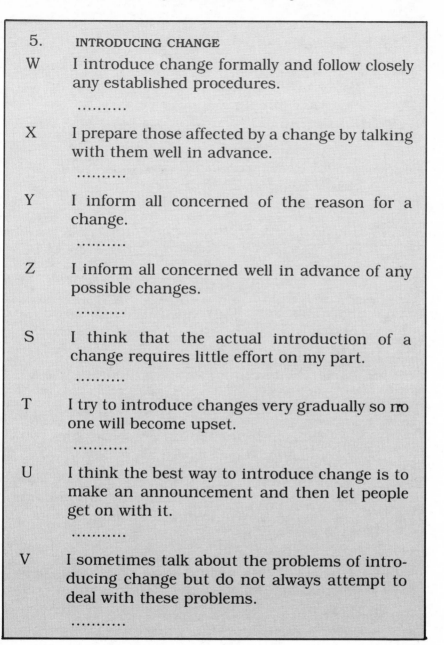

5. INTRODUCING CHANGE

W   I introduce change formally and follow closely any established procedures.

    ....

X   I prepare those affected by a change by talking with them well in advance.

    ....

Y   I inform all concerned of the reason for a change.

    ....

Z   I inform all concerned well in advance of any possible changes.

    ....

S   I think that the actual introduction of a change requires little effort on my part.

    ....

T   I try to introduce changes very gradually so no one will become upset.

    ....

U   I think the best way to introduce change is to make an announcement and then let people get on with it.

    ....

V   I sometimes talk about the problems of introducing change but do not always attempt to deal with these problems.

    ....

Distribute ten points over not more than four statements to indicate the degree to which the statements reflect your own management style. You may allocate all ten points to one statement, or five to each of two, or in any other way. Do not assign points to more than four statements.

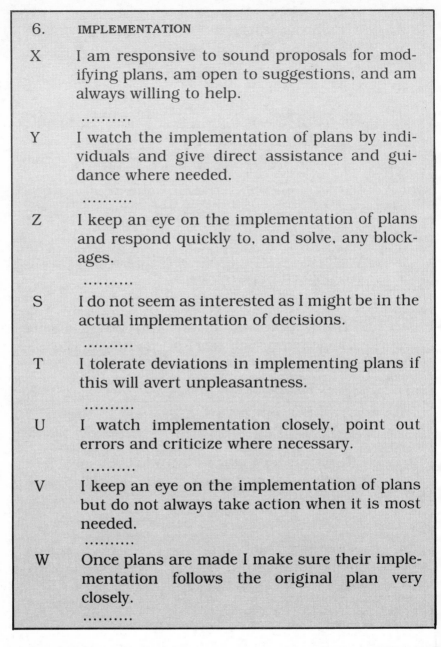

6. **IMPLEMENTATION**

X   I am responsive to sound proposals for modifying plans, am open to suggestions, and am always willing to help.

....

Y   I watch the implementation of plans by individuals and give direct assistance and guidance where needed.

....

Z   I keep an eye on the implementation of plans and respond quickly to, and solve, any blockages.

....

S   I do not seem as interested as I might be in the actual implementation of decisions.

....

T   I tolerate deviations in implementing plans if this will avert unpleasantness.

....

U   I watch implementation closely, point out errors and criticize where necessary.

....

V   I keep an eye on the implementation of plans but do not always take action when it is most needed.

....

W   Once plans are made I make sure their implementation follows the original plan very closely.

....

Distribute ten points over not more than four statements to indicate the degree to which the statements reflect your own management style. You may allocate all ten points to one statement, or five to each of two, or in any other way. Do not assign points to more than four statements.

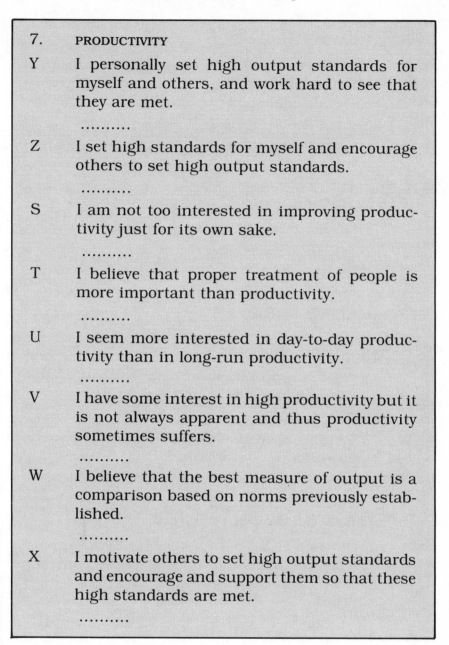

7.	**PRODUCTIVITY**
Y	I personally set high output standards for myself and others, and work hard to see that they are met.
	....
Z	I set high standards for myself and encourage others to set high output standards.
	....
S	I am not too interested in improving productivity just for its own sake.
	....
T	I believe that proper treatment of people is more important than productivity.
	....
U	I seem more interested in day-to-day productivity than in long-run productivity.
	....
V	I have some interest in high productivity but it is not always apparent and thus productivity sometimes suffers.
	....
W	I believe that the best measure of output is a comparison based on norms previously established.
	....
X	I motivate others to set high output standards and encourage and support them so that these high standards are met.
	....

Distribute ten points over not more than four statements to indicate the degree to which the statements reflect your own management style. You may allocate all ten points to one statement, or five to each of two, or in any other way. Do not assign points to more than four statements.

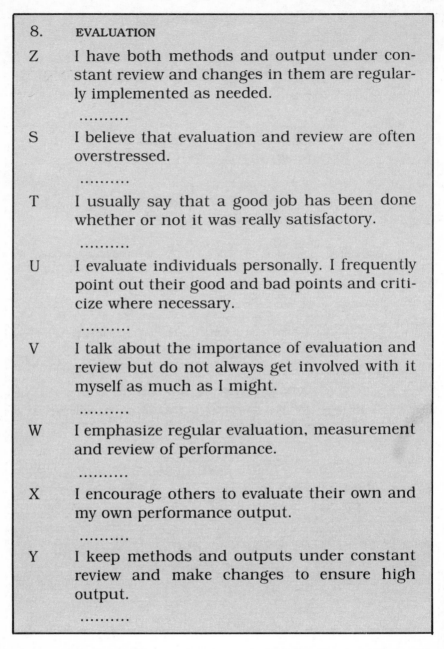

8.   **EVALUATION**

Z   I have both methods and output under constant review and changes in them are regularly implemented as needed.

....

S   I believe that evaluation and review are often overstressed.

....

T   I usually say that a good job has been done whether or not it was really satisfactory.

....

U   I evaluate individuals personally. I frequently point out their good and bad points and criticize where necessary.

....

V   I talk about the importance of evaluation and review but do not always get involved with it myself as much as I might.

....

W   I emphasize regular evaluation, measurement and review of performance.

....

X   I encourage others to evaluate their own and my own performance output.

....

Y   I keep methods and outputs under constant review and make changes to ensure high output.

....

Distribute ten points over not more than four statements to indicate the degree to which the statements reflect your own management style. You may allocate all ten points to one statement, or five to each of two, or in any other way. Do not assign points to more than four statements.

INVENTORY SUMMARY

3-D		Creativity	Data Collection	Setting Objectives	Planning	Introducing Change	Implementation	Productivity	Evaluation
		1	2	3	4	5	6	7	8
Z									
V									
Y									
U									
X									
T									
W									
S									

TOTAL = 80

PROFILE CHART

From the Inventory Summary on page 181, transfer your style scores to the boxes for each style and then shade or hatch in the profile chart. This will be used again for your overall profile in Chapter 15.

	0–5	6–10	11–15	16–20	21–25	26–30	31–35	36–40	41–45	46+
Executive Z ☐										
Compromiser V ☐										
Ben. Autocrat Y ☐										
Autocrat U ☐										
Developer X ☐										
Missionary T ☐										
Bureaucrat W ☐										
Deserter S ☐										

WHAT IS BEING MEASURED?

You may have more or less one dominant style for each of the elements in this test. It is more likely, however, that you behave with some elements in some ways and with other elements in other ways. This of course relates to varying levels of effectiveness with different elements. You may want to think about, and possibly discuss with your spouse or a colleague, why the differences arise. The basic question is, as always, is it you or your situation?

EIGHT MANAGERIAL STYLES

Each basic style has its more effective and less effective counterpart, as demonstrated in Figure 12.1. The eight styles which reflect the effectiveness level are called managerial styles to distinguish them from the four basic styles. The two basic dimensions are still task orientation (TO) and relationships orientation (RO). The third dimension is managerial effectiveness (E), or the extent to which a manager achieves the output requirements of the position.

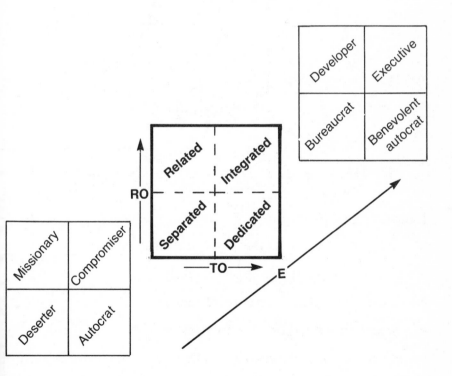

Figure 12.1. The 3-D style model
The complete 3-D style model consists of four basic styles, four more effective managerial styles, and four less effective managerial styles.

Z. Executive

The executive manager is one who is using high task orientation and high relationships orientation in a situation where such behaviour is appropriate and who is therefore more effective.

Figure 12.2. The executive manager

Executive indicators

- Uses teamwork in decision making
- Uses participation appropriately
- Induces commitment to objectives
- Encourages higher performance
- Co-ordinates others in work.

V. Compromiser

The compromiser manager is one who is using high task orientation and high relationships orientation in a situation that requires high orientation to only one or neither and who is therefore less effective.

Figure 12.3. The compromiser

Compromiser indicators

- Over-uses participation
- Yielding/weak
- Avoids decisions
- Produces grey acceptable decisions
- Idealist/ambiguous
- Sometimes encourages new ideas but does not always follow up on too many of them.

Y. Benevolent autocrat

The benevolent autocrat manager is one who is using high task orientation and low relationships orientation in a situation where such behaviour is appropriate and who is therefore more effective.

Figure 12.4. The benevolent autocrat

Benevolent autocrat indicators

- Decisive/shows initiative
- Industrious/energetic
- Finisher/committed
- Evaluative of quantity, quality and time
- Cost, profit and sales conscious
- Obtains results
- Both develops and proposes many new ideas
- Shows that efficiency and productivity are valued.

U. Autocrat

The autocrat manager is one who is using high task orientation and low relationships orientation in a situation where such behaviour is inappropriate and who is therefore less effective.

Figure 12.5. The autocrat

Autocrat indicators

- Critical/threatening

- Makes decisions

- Demands obedience/suppresses conflict

- Wants action and results immediately

- Downward communication only

- Acts without consultation

- Feared/disliked

- More interested in day-to-day productivity than in long-run productivity

- Performance maintained through subtle threatening situation.

X. Developer

The developer manager is one who is using high relationships orientation and low task orientation in a situation where such behaviour is appropriate and who is therefore more effective.

Figure 12.6. The developer

Developer indicators

- Maintains open communication channels
- Develops talent of others/coaches
- Understands others/supports
- Works well with others/co-operates
- Trusted by others/trusts/listens
- When responsible for planning, involves many others.

T. Missionary

The missionary manager is one who is using high relationships orientation and low task orientation in a situation where such behaviour is inappropriate and who is therefore less effective.

Figure 12.7. The missionary

Missionary indicators

- Avoids conflict
- Pleasant/kind/warm
- Seeks acceptance of self/dependent
- Makes things easier
- Avoids initiation/passive/gives no direction
- Unconcerned with outputs and standards
- At first sign of conflict attempts to smooth.

W. Bureaucrat

The bureaucrat manager is one who is using low task orientation and low relationships orientation in a situation where such behaviour is appropriate and who is therefore more effective.

Figure 12.8. The bureaucrat

Bureaucrat indicators

- Follows orders, rules, procedures
- Reliable/dependable
- Maintains system and going concerns
- Watches details/efficient
- Rational/logical/self-controlled
- Fair/just/equitable
- Prefers to write out communications with others
- Responds to disagreement and conflict by referring to rules and procedures.

S. Deserter

The deserter manager is one who is using low task orientation and low relationships orientation in a situation where such behaviour is inappropriate and who is therefore less effective.

Figure 12.9. The deserter

Deserter indicators

- Works to rules/minimum output/gives up
- Avoids involvement and responsibility
- Gives few useful opinions or suggestions
- Uncreative/unoriginal/narrow-minded
- Hinders others/makes things difficult
- Resists change/unco-operative
- Shows little concern about errors and usually does little to correct or reduce them.

Output—oriented organizations are quiet places in which to work. Input—oriented organizations lead to heart attacks and ulcers.

WJR

It is impossible to appraise a manager without knowing the output requirements of the position.

WJR

Chapter 13

Organization Output Survey

INTRODUCTION

Outputs are defined as things to be achieved.

INSTRUCTIONS

Consider each item in relation to how you would best describe your current situation against each of the statements.

Circle or check either disagree or agree in each and every case.

1	My superior and I regularly agree on my outputs.	
	Disagree	Agree
2	I have most of the people I need in order to perform effectively.	
	Disagree	Agree
3	I have reached agreement with my subordinates on how their effectiveness will be measured.	
	Disagree	Agree
4	More emphasis on output orientation would improve my effectiveness.	
	Disagree	Agree
5	I have worked out directly with my subordinates what both they and I are responsible for.	
	Disagree	Agree

(6) I welcome output orientation.

Disagree		Agree

(7) Most of the job-related information I receive comes in good time.

Disagree		Agree

(8) I discuss my subordinates' less effective performance with them.

Disagree		Agree

(9) Most of the job-related information I receive is accurate enough.

Disagree		Agree

(10) My superior and I have agreed how my effectiveness should be measured.

Disagree		Agree

(11) My outputs link with the outputs of those I work with at my level.

Disagree		Agree

(12) My superior has a strong interest in how effective I am.

Disagree		Agree

(13) I think output orientation is welcomed by my superior.

Disagree		Agree

(14) There is effective inter-unit co-operation here.

Disagree		Agree

(15) My superior discusses my less effective performance with me.

Disagree		Agree

16 More emphasis on output orientation would improve my subordinates' effectiveness.

Disagree | | Agree

17 I discuss my subordinates' outputs with them rather than give them duties to carry out.

Disagree | | Agree

18 My superior usually tells me how effective I am.

Disagree | | Agree

19 My authority is clearly defined.

Disagree | | Agree

20 My subordinates participate fully with me in setting the outputs for their positions.

Disagree | | Agree

21 I have most of the equipment I need in order to perform effectively.

Disagree | | Agree

22 As much as they can, my co-workers help me to become more effective.

Disagree | | Agree

23 I think output orientation would be welcomed by those below me.

Disagree | | Agree

24 I have sufficient authority to achieve what is expected of me.

Disagree | | Agree

25 I think output orientation is welcomed by top management.

Disagree | | Agree

26	I can get most of the job-related information I need fairly easily.	
	Disagree	Agree

27	I have had most of the training I need in order to perform effectively.	
	Disagree	Agree

28	As much as I can, I regularly help my co-workers to become more effective.	
	Disagree	Agree

29	I have most of the space I need in order to perform effectively.	
	Disagree	Agree

30	My outputs link with those of my superior.	
	Disagree	Agree

31	More emphasis on output orientation would improve my superior's effectiveness.	
	Disagree	Agree

32	I have a job description which is helpful to me in setting outputs.	
	Disagree	Agree

33	I can influence the outputs of my superior.	
	Disagree	Agree

34	I have most of the budget I need in order to perform effectively.	
	Disagree	Agree

35	Most of the job-related information I receive is useful to me.	
	Disagree	Agree

36 | I have a job description which is reasonably up-to-date and accurate.

Disagree | | Agree

37 | More emphasis on output orientation would improve my co-workers' effectiveness.

Disagree | | Agree

38 | I can usually change my authority and responsibility if I make a good case.

Disagree | | Agree

39 | I think output orientation would have many benefits here.

Disagree | | Agree

40 | I receive all the job-related information I need to perform effectively.

Disagree | | Agree

41 | My responsibility and authority fit well with those of my superior.

Disagree | | Agree

42 | More emphasis on output orientation would improve this organization's effectiveness.

Disagree | | Agree

43 | I have most of the assistance from my superior I need in order to perform effectively.

Disagree | | Agree

44 | I discuss regularly with my subordinates how effective they are.

Disagree | | Agree

45 | My responsibility and authority fit well with those of my subordinates.

Disagree | | Agree

(46) I think output orientation would lead to some effective changes.

Disagree | | Agree

(47) I help to make my superior more effective.

Disagree | | Agree

(48) I have most of the assistance I need from my subordinates in order to perform effectively.

Disagree | | Agree

(49) Most meetings I attend here are productive.

Disagree | | Agree

(50) I can use most of the job-related information I receive.

Disagree | | Agree

(51) My responsibility and authority fit well with those of my co-workers.

Disagree | | Agree

(52) Much of the job-related information I am required to produce seems to be of value.

Disagree | | Agree

(53) I have most of the assistance from my co-workers I need in order to perform effectively.

Disagree | | Agree

(54) I am encouraged to interact directly with my co-workers without going through my superior or their superiors.

Disagree | | Agree

(55) I have most of the specialist advice I need in order to perform effectively.

Disagree | | Agree

56 Most of the job-related information I get seems to reflect reality.

Disagree		Agree

57 My subordinates are responsible to me.

Disagree		Agree

58 Change is easily introduced here.

Disagree		Agree

59 I am responsible to my superior.

Disagree		Agree

60 More emphasis on output orientation would reduce conflict here.

Disagree		Agree

61 I meet regularly with my subordinates to agree on their outputs.

Disagree		Agree

62 I receive the information I need in order to judge my effectiveness.

Disagree		Agree

63 I have most of the information I need in order to perform effectively.

Disagree		Agree

64 My outputs link with those of my subordinates.

Disagree		Agree

65 More emphasis on output orientation would improve job satisfaction here.

Disagree		Agree

66 I help to make my subordinates more effective.

| Disagree | | Agree |

67 More emphasis on output orientation would enable me to work more effectively with my superior.

| Disagree | | Agree |

68 My superior and I discuss any blockages between us.

| Disagree | | Agree |

69 Useful informal meetings are often held here.

| Disagree | | Agree |

70 Change is often introduced here.

| Disagree | | Agree |

71 My superior helps me to become more effective.

| Disagree | | Agree |

72 This organization is highly flexible.

| Disagree | | Agree |

73 I receive the information I need in order to judge my subordinates' effectiveness.

| Disagree | | Agree |

74 My subordinates and I discuss blockages between us and remove them.

| Disagree | | Agree |

75 More emphasis on output orientation would enable me to work more effectively with my subordinates.

| Disagree | | Agree |

76 My responsibility and authority fit well with those of my co-workers.

Disagree		Agree

77 Changes can be introduced quickly and effectively here.

Disagree		Agree

78 I allow others to bypass my authority and responsibility as long as effectiveness is maintained.

Disagree		Agree

79 More emphasis on output orientation would enable me to work more effectively with my co-workers.

Disagree		Agree

80 My co-workers and I discuss blockages between us and remove them.

Disagree		Agree

HOW TO CALCULATE YOUR SCORE

A. To calculate your score for the first scale being measured, circle each item number that you agreed with. Enter the number of circles in the score box against that scale on the profile chart on page 181.

B. Then do this for the other seven scales.

Scale: *Effective linking with superior*

The degree to which the superior is seen using outputs and effectiveness as a means of managing.

1, 10, 12, 15, 18, 30, 33, 47, 68, 71.

Scale: *Effective linking with subordinates*

The degree to which oneself is using elements of output orientation with subordinates.

3, 5, 8, 17, 20, 44, 61, 64, 66, 74.

Scale: *Effective linking with co-workers*

The degree to which the relationship with co-workers facilitates the output process.

11, 14, 22, 28, 49, 54, 69, 76, 78, 80.

Scale: *authority and effective position design*

The degree to which one sees authority in the position as being clearly and appropriately designed.

19, 24, 32, 36, 38, 41, 45, 51, 57, 59.

Scale: Resources to position

The degree to which there are sufficient resources available to perform effectively.

2, 21, 27, 29, 34, 43, 48, 53, 55, 63.

Scale: Climate for output orientation

The degree to which the climate is ready for output orientation.

6, 13, 23, 25, 39, 46, 58, 70, 72, 77.

Scale: Benefits of output orientation

The degree to which output orientation has potential benefits.

4, 16, 31, 37, 42, 60, 65, 67, 75, 79.

Scale: Effective management information

The degree to which the management information system is seen as adequate.

7, 9, 26, 35, 40, 50, 52, 56, 62, 73.

PROFILE CHART

Shade or hatch in your score on the profile chart below. This will be used again for your overall profile in Chapter 15.

	1	2	3	4	5	6	7	8	9	10
Effective Linking with Superior										
Effective Linking with Subordinates										
Effective Linking with Co-workers										
Authority and Effective Position Design										
Resources to Position										
Climate for Output Orientation										
Benefits of Output Orientation										
Effective Management Information										

This Test was designed by W. J. Reddin
© W. J. Reddin, 1991.

This Test is copyright in all countries and it is illegal to photocopy it. Copies may be obtained from the addresses given in Chapter 20.

Part III: Thinking About Your Scores

This part of the book is designed to show you how to make the best use of your results. It is one thing to have completed the tests; it is quite another thing to make the best use of what you found out about yourself.

Management must develop as broad a horizon as possible for every position, with guide posts along the way rather than rigid fences that hem the individual into a completely preplanned . . . existence.

Edward C. Schleh

People move in the course of their daily work from a role in one system to a different role in another system; and it is essential that this be recognized and the behaviour appropriate to the role be adopted if trouble is to be avoided.

Wilfred Brown

Chapter 14

Your Four Managerial Skills

INTRODUCTION

You are a manager in a particular situation. You know that managerial effectiveness results from a match of your behaviour to the situation. If you behave inappropriately, possibly because you are serving your own needs, you will be less effective. If you behave appropriately because you can read the situation well and act correspondingly, you will be more effective. From this can be derived the four absolutely key managerial skills:

- Self-awareness skill

- Situational sensitivity skill

- Style flexibility skill

- Situational management skill

This book has been designed to sharply increase your self-awareness skill. This surely must be the first of the four skills, because if you do not know how you are behaving or why you are behaving that way you are clearly likely to be less effective. The acquisition of the four skills is sometimes learnt naturally and is therefore called experience. It is absolutely certain that all these skills can be increased by reading clearly written books and attending well-designed managerial seminars on which those books are based.

The remainder of this chapter is based on further explanation of each of these skills. Chapter 17 shows how to put them into practice by applying what you have learnt about yourself in completing this book so far.

SELF-AWARENESS SKILL

A first step towards improving our situational sensitivity is to improve our self-awareness. Self-awareness is the degree to which managers can appraise their own style correctly. It is knowledge of our impact on others, not of our impact on ourselves. The prime usefulness of this self-knowledge is to enable managers to make a more effective impact on the situation, not so that they can marvel at their own psychic interior.

Effective managers must know the impact they are having on others. Without this knowledge, they cannot assess the situation they are in and cannot predict the results of their own behaviour. Many types of group-dynamic management training courses attempt to, and usually can, improve self-awareness – as can a spouse or even children.

Four parts of self

Everything known and not known about ourselves can be placed under one of the following headings:

1. What we know and others know (self-awareness)
   (This is everybody's business)

2. What others know and we do not know (self-unawareness)
   (We must make this our business)

3. What we know and others do not know (personal history)
   (This is our business only)

4. What we and others do not know (unconsciousness)
   (This is no one's business).

These can be arranged as demonstrated in Figure 14.1. The idea on which this Figure is based (only some terminology is changed) was developed by two psychologists, Joe Luft and Harry Ingham, who call it the Johari Window.

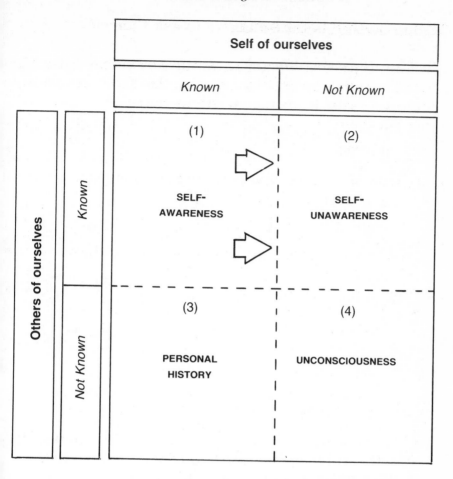

Figure 14.1. Four parts of self

This diagram sharpens the importance of decreasing our degree of self-unawareness. The self-unawareness area is that part of our behaviour which others are well aware of but we are not. In simple terms, we may be acting in ways towards others, perhaps rejecting them, of which we are essentially unaware. Clearly, to be effective with others we must know just what kind of impact we are making. To become more effective, then, a manager needs to make window (2) smaller by increasing the size of window (1).

Without a reasonable degree of self-awareness, it is difficult to use 3-D concepts. Without knowing our own basic self, it is all too easy to distort the style of another or the basic style demands of a situation itself.

Some questions for managers to ask themselves

Self-awareness is difficult to improve by simply thinking about it, but some assistance may be obtained by answering each of the following questions honestly.

1. If someone said of you, 'You sometimes act like a kid', what behaviour would they be thinking of?

2. What do you do that gets you into trouble?

3. Are there any major themes in your life which seem to repeat themselves, perhaps in different contexts?

4. Do you care more about yourself than others?

5. If you obtained a pension you could live off today, would you still like to keep your job?

6. What did you do when your father was angry with you? When your mother was angry with you? When your friends were angry with you?

7. What does your spouse think of you? What do your children think of you?

8. What do you do when your superior is angry with you? When your subordinates are angry with you? When your co-workers are angry with you?

9. What typically do you do when under attack or faced with conflict?

10. What are your major disappointments in life?

11. What are your major disappointments at work?

12. Who is responsible for your major disappointments?

13. What made you proudest as a child? As an adult?

14. What is your favourite day dream? Do you see anything in it that might be making you a more or less effective manager?

15. What is your single major accomplishment?

Most of these questions tap the manager's underlying personality dynamics. They are questions which we seldom think about. The answers to them differentiate ourselves sharply from others.

As you can gather, a major objective of this book is to greatly improve your self-awareness skill.

SITUATIONAL SENSITIVITY SKILL

A key managerial skill is the ability to size up a situation. A manager with the sensitivity to read a situation for what it actually contains, and the sensitivity to know what behaviour would actually constitute effectiveness in it, is likely to be effective. Situational sensitivity is the ability to read situations correctly for what they really contain.

Age and experience tend to improve situational sensitivity, as this skill is a component of experience. However, young managers just out of college sometimes show a brilliant understanding of situations and of what must be done to produce effectiveness. They know when to push hard, when not to, whom to see, and the appropriate timing. The sensitive manager will know what resistances stand in the way of being effective and what can and what must be overcome to be effective. Although situational sensitivity is seldom perfect, managers can learn ways to improve this.

Sensitivity requires intellectual alertness and curiosity. The sensitive manager fits scraps of information and hunches together. As with the work of any social scientist, the whole can be constructed by looking at the detail. From a firebed and arrowhead, an anthropologist constructs a civilization. From the way in which a policy is received from different divisions, a sensitive manager can construct the reality of power politics in an organization.

Situational sensitivity is a particularly useful skill when dealing with other departments. As often occurs in such situations, managers have no real power. They must elicit co-operation, based on mutual understanding. Managers are more likely to be effective if they pay some attention to the realities and fantasies of how each department operates, who the key people are, where the power really lies; while it is useful, sensitivity is not such a crucial skill in stable or highly structured environments. When managers have trained for years for particular kinds of unchanging situations, their need for sensitivity decreases. In some circumstances, sensitivity may even be a hindrance because the manager may be acutely aware of what is required yet be unable to do anything about it. For the new person in any position, situational sensitivity is crucial. It is a must to know the answer to the question, 'What does it take to be effective here?'

Do not trust to luck

Many highly sensitive managers, politicians or, for that matter, entrepreneurs are often described as lucky. The term 'luck', like magic, is really simply a device to explain what is to some people an otherwise inexplicable outcome. Luck seldom explains managerial effectiveness. The manager in the right place at the right time with the appropriate resources did not get there solely by chance, although it may appear that way. Such managers very often understood the existing or potential situation and were prepared for the opportunities as they came.

Although skill in situational sensitivity varies widely from manager to manager, it can be improved by experience and training and by an understanding of the reasons which lead all of us to distort the real world.

Situational insensitivity

For a variety of reasons, unconsciously, we are sometimes not interested in making a sound situational diagnosis. It may be that if we made a realistic diagnosis we would discover things we do not like, or things that we simply do not want to know, or things that we do not know how to handle. The main, unconscious mental protective

devices we use are known as defence mechanisms origi-
nally proposed by Sigmund Freud. The main defence
mechanisms that managers should be aware of in themselves and others are rationalization (inventing reasons)
and projection (its you, not me).

Defence mechanisms are not necessarily psychological-
ly unhealthy; all healthy personalities need temporary
protection from time to time. The problem occurs when
the temporary protection turns into a permanent drop in
situational sensitivity, to a distortion of reality.

Defence mechanisms operate entirely outside the manager's awareness. They operate in the unconscious. They
serve to hide or to shield that person from what is
unacceptable, threatening or repugnant in the situation,
so that these things become unrecognized or unacknow-
ledged. In layman's language, defence mechanisms give
us blind spots that unconsciously, we think we need.

Rationalization (inventing reasons)

Rationalization involves inventing and accepting inter-
pretations which an impartial analysis would not sub-
stantiate; it is deluding ourselves about what the world is
really like. Rationalization serves to conceal motives and
impulses that are unacceptable. It also serves to construct our view of the situation in such a way that the
problem is in the situation, not in ourselves. The jus-
tification of such an interpretation usually involves giving socially acceptable reasons for behaviour or apparently logical reasons for the view of the situation. In business
life, what is rationalized in this way is usually believed by
the manager but is often not believed or understood by
the listener.

All managers are familiar with rationalization. They see
it in the manager passed over for promotion who decided
not to want it anyway. This is known as 'sour grapes'
(after the fable about the fox who could not get at some
grapes and who then decided they were sour anyway).
Managers who continually 'sour grape' may turn into one.

Managers transferred against their wishes may later find that they like their new jobs. This is known as 'sweet lemon', to suggest that we invest an unpleasant object or event with positive references when it is forced on us. It is clear that at times rationalization is an excellent adaptive mechanism which enables us to meet negative circumstances. The change in opinion, of course, may be real and based on objective reality. In this case this is not rationalization but factual reappraisal.

Managers who are consistently late with their reports find many ways to rationalize their behaviour. They may blame subordinates, overwork, or unanticipated problems. For none of these delays do they feel they can be held responsible. The real reasons may be fear of being evaluated by the report, unconsciously wanting to inconvenience report recipients, or simply incompetence. These real reasons are not known to them: if they knew them and still put excuses forward, they are not rationalizing – they are lying.

Rationalization is not rare. Whereas some managers use it so much that it incapacitates them, most use it to some degree: 'The job was not completed because other things came up', 'The promotion was missed because the superior was biased', 'The subordinate was fired because of incompetence'.

Ordinary levels of rationalization cannot be regarded as serious, but over-use can assume exaggerated proportions. An incompetent manager with a high need for achievement and an excessive fear of failure might easily develop almost pathological rationalizations, perhaps leading to delusion of persecution. Managers like this might believe that their superiors 'have it in for them'. This rationalization may protect them from facing the real reasons for failure and lack of promotion. The over-use of rationalization may so remove managers from their real problems that they may end up with a crisis that cannot be solved. If we 'save face' too much we may simply end up without a true identity.

Rationalization is sometimes excusable on the grounds that it eases the shock of an unpleasant situation. It softens our misgivings about ourselves, eases our conscience, and enables us to reconstruct reality slowly so that it does not affront our views of ourselves. Some would say that if we did not rationalize we would go crazy, and there is truth in this for less effective managers. For the effective manager, however, there is no substitute for reading a situation clearly, facing it squarely, and dealing with it realistically.

The problem with rationalization is not so much that we delude ourselves but that it provides no guidelines for appropriate action. The essential ingredient of rationalization is distortion to protect ourselves. This distorted perception leads to the identification of the wrong elements to change. Typically, managers who are rationalizing may want to change others or perhaps the technology, when really they should be changing themselves.

University students who do not participate enough in case-study classes usually have a set of rationalizations to explain their behaviour. These include, 'Too many people talk with nothing to say', 'Still waters run deep', 'We should have a public speaking course' and even, 'I was quiet when I was a child'.

The best indicator to rationalization in ourselves or others is the too perfect, too logical, or too consistent explanation. Life is fairly complex, and somewhat tentative explanations are what usually we must use. Rationalization, however, is usually a logical masterpiece – all the bits fit together to make a perfect cover-up story. Another clue is the insistence with which the rationalization is offered as an explanation. Shakespeare illuminated this with 'The lady doth protest too much methinks'. Winston Churchill was said to have sometimes written in the margin of his speeches 'weak point – shout'.

Projection (it's you, not me)

Projection is seeing in others what we do not want to see and cannot see in ourselves. It operates primarily in those with low self-awareness – those who do not know how they, in fact, behave.

The mechanism is most clearly seen in delusions of persecution. For example, new managers may be in the process of making changes in their departments, but not all subordinates will like change, and each will react somewhat differently. Some subordinates might feel aggressive towards their new manager but, because of their social training, they may not express it or even be aware of it in themselves. By the mechanism of projection, they then may suspect their manager of having these feelings towards them or, as an extreme, believe they are victims of a conspiracy.

Such statements as these may reveal projection at work: 'The production department is not to be trusted', 'They are wolves in sheep's clothing' and 'Everyone has their price'.

Projection may be combined with rationalization, with undesirable results. Some managers who cannot accept and do not see the hostility in themselves may project this on to others and see them as mean and aggressive. They may then have to rationalize why they act this way towards others. They develop a belief that they want the other person's job and so are trying to get that person fired.

Typical examples of projection are the slacker who sees others as lazy, the selfish person who complains that others do not share, or managers with low relationships orientation who are concerned that no one seems to take an interest in them. University students often project their unconscious feelings about their instructors on to the instructors themselves. They say the instructors do not like them and are being personal, when the opposite (but unacceptable to them) condition is true.

Projection is costly to managerial effectiveness because it can be maintained only at the cost of continually misperceiving social reality. Although such distortion is designed unconsciously to protect the manager, in the long run the effect may be the opposite.

Hate at first sight

One indicator of low situational sensitivity is having a tendency to take an instinctive dislike to some people. There are many natural and obvious reasons why this might occur but some people make a habit of it. Why might you take an instinctive dislike to someone, perhaps a new work colleague, you have never really known? There are three main reasons for this kind of irrational response. It might be that the person reminds you of someone you dislike, or displays a quality which you dislike in yourself, or is in some way a threat to your security. This threat to your security may be anything from making higher performance demands on you, showing you up at work in some way just by simply being more effective, or bringing in some pressure for you to change your comfortable work habits.

Appraising situational sensitivity

If managers make a series of interventions in situations which prove effective, it is highly probable that they have a high sensitivity to situations. If not, they would have made the wrong moves. If managers do nothing, however, this alone does not indicate whether or not they have high or low sensitivity. They may know what is wrong but not know how to do anything about it.

Situational sensitivity is a diagnostic not an action skill. This simply means that a manager may score high on the situational sensitivity scale, and yet do nothing with the skill possessed. The well-trained psychologist, sociologist or anthropologist may have the highest possible situational sensitivity yet the lowest possible effectiveness as a manager. To be effective, the sensitivity must be

217

matched with one, but preferably both, of either style flexibility or situational management skill.

Management training exercises are available which measure situational sensitivity with great precision. They consist of depicting a situation by a film or written case study and then asking the manager to make a series of observations concerning it.

Situational sensitivity alone

Situational sensitivity alone is of little value to the practising manager. If managers cannot use what they already know, they might as well not know it. Those who go through life as hostile or only as friendly observers of the scene are serving some need to appear intellectual rather than to be useful and, therefore, effective. People do not like to feel they are being analyzed, and this is what situational sensitivity alone can lead to.

Sensitivity must be related to an action programme of either managerial flexibility or situation management. Some managers have high sensitivity but low flexibility. They tend to change situations rather than change themselves. They use situational management.

STYLE FLEXIBILITY SKILL

Flexible managers are perceived as having few personal needs or biases which may lead them to interpret wrongly the real world. They are reality oriented and this reality guides their actions. They are not led to analyze a situation in terms of how they think things *should* be. Rather, they read a situation for what it is and for what can reasonably be accomplished. They are seldom identified with lost causes but more often with objectives being achieved. Flexible managers are essentially optimistic about themselves and about situations. Often they see things they do not care for but know that with time and appropriate behaviour a situation can be changed.

Because flexible managers recognize that they live in a complex world, they are aware that in order to be effective in it a wide range of responses is necessary. Flexible managers are very sensitive to other people. They are not only sensitive to their differences but accept the differences as normal, appropriate, and even necessary. Flexible managers are trusted, and all believe that their proposals for change are based on improving overall effectiveness and are not intended simply to satisfy their own needs in some way.

Flexible managers spend more time in making decisions and less time in implementing them. They are concerned with methods of introduction, timing, rate of introduction, and probable responses and resistances. In spending more time on devising how to implement decisions, the implementation period is shortened considerably. Snap decisions are seldom made. Flexible managers use team management when appropriate, which gives them an ideal opportunity to use their flexibility.

Rapid change does not make them unduly anxious. It brings temporary ambiguity which flexible managers can tolerate easily. They are likely to be willing to experiment with changes that have only a moderate chance of success. They know that the world is complex; they recognize that any change may bring unanticipated consequences, so they are prepared to test a large number of ideas.

Flexible managers are willing to accept a variety of styles of management, varying degrees of participation, and an assortment of control techniques. Appropriateness is their only test. During the course of a few hours they may have used a variety of basic styles; they adapt their style to what is then demanded. They use participation at times, and at others they do not.

Style flexibility checklist

Reality-oriented	Colleague-oriented
Optimistic	Fair
Objective	Situationist (looks outward)
Other-directed	Adaptive

219

Sensitive	Open-minded
Collaborative	Socially adjusted
Tolerant	Experimental
Interdependent	Participative at times
Involved	Uses all basic styles
Team player	Practical

The four personality characteristics which underlie flexible behaviour include:

- High ambiguity tolerance (comfortable in unstructured situations)

- Power insensitivity (not control-oriented)

- Open belief system (few fixed ideas)

- Other-directed (interested in others).

High ambiguity tolerance

Flexible people have a high tolerance for ambiguity. They are comfortable in an unstructured situation where one or more of the past, present or future are ill-defined. They are not too threatened by rapid, unexpected changes. They are not drawn to paperwork as they see this as unnecessarily structuring a situation best kept loose. They favour short reports, loose ground rules, and open-ended planning and scheduling. It is important for them to maintain a friendly, easy atmosphere where the 'old network' approach is used more than 'standard operating procedures'. Approaches that could be characterized as 'right or wrong', 'black or white', 'go/no-go', and 'win/lose' are foreign to the flexible manager.

Power insensitivity

Being insensitive to power often leads these managers to listen more to subordinates than to their superiors. They generally favour flattening the status and power differences between levels and usually avoid displays of status symbols. They are in favour of most forms of participation. Flexible managers are sensitive to the way things are. They see good management as the art of the possible. They would prefer things to develop and flow naturally rather than go one step at a time or be dramatically restructured.

Open belief system

Flexible managers are open-minded. They are ready to see new points of view and to expose themselves to influence. They could easily hold a particular view on one day and change their minds, in the light of new evidence, a day later. They are more concerned with full knowledge than in having their prior beliefs confirmed. They are less likely than others to take extreme positions for or against anything. They have a capacity to accommodate a wide range of viewpoints and do not feel they must make a successful synthesis of them.

Even when unable to accept another point of view, flexible managers will always listen to it, usually contemplate it seriously, and often live comfortably with it although it may be contradictory to their existing belief system. They are usually open to new inputs from any source. They are continually searching for maximum contact with their environment and are thus open to influence. This openness leads them to discard prior methods with ease. Not tending to hold extreme, fixed views, they argue less vehemently than others. They are tolerant of others holding opposite views. If they have to change their minds, they can do so easily, and are therefore as much interested in hearing other views as in pushing their own.

To have flexibility, managers must have few, if any, intrusive personal needs. They must not need to do things in one particular way, to have a particular relationship with others, to live according to a particular ideology or to accomplish a particular thing.

Other-directed

Their openness to influence and their unconcern with power mean that the flexible type are team members. They want to be involved in analysis, planning and decision making with others. They seek collaboration with their co-workers and are willing to accommodate a group view rather than maintain their own. Thus they are usually more prepared to work for a consensus decision than for a vote. They look for that creative solution or synthesis that everyone will accept. In fact, they find it a challenge to work for a solution which combines all views, even though the final decision may have some ambiguous element.

Flexible managers tend to get involved with people as individuals, not just as subordinates or co-workers. They do not see others as bounded by their role. They are sensitive to individual differences and want to respond to them. They sometimes find themselves involved with other managers' home problems — this is not because they are inquisitive or have relationships orientation but because they are interested in a variety of inputs, and thus look at the total person rather than at a human frame bounded by a job description.

SITUATIONAL MANAGEMENT SKILL

To improve their effectiveness, managers need not only to practise situational management but also to be sensitive to the results, in terms of effectiveness, of the situational management action taken.

Feedback loops

To obtain feedback on the effectiveness of situational management it is necessary to be highly sensitive as to what the true effects of the situational management exercise actually was. Chapter 17 provides several ideas for improving your effectiveness. Some you will try, some you will not. Those you try have to be monitored in terms of results, in terms of your effectiveness.

Your feedback loop may be simply a candid subordinate who tells the manager quickly when things are unacceptable. The loop may also be a measurement of a production process that needs involvement and teamwork to keep it going. Effective managers cultivate short-term feedback loops so they can get quick readings on the effect of their actions. Psychologists have shown, in a variety of experiments, that performance improves when the results of performance are known. To put it more directly, without feedback there is little learning. To improve our style, we must have feedback on its effect.

Feedback loops are built into many types of technical systems. They are designed to provide corrections to the planned course. Such loops keep guided missiles on target or radio receivers on frequency. When the actual events vary from those planned, they provide a means of correcting the deviation.

Grapevine and rumour are forms of feedback. While both tend to be quick, they also tend to distort reality.

Figure 14.2 has six steps. The sixth step leads into repetition of the cycle.

1. A situational diagnosis is made.

2. The manager decides on a situational management technique.

3. The manager takes action.

4. The manager obtains feedback on the results of the action. Without this step, the feedback-learning cycle cannot continue. This is its weakest link since it depends on the climate the manager has created and skill in listening and observing.

5. The manager evaluates the effectiveness of the action, and then decides whether it led to more or less effectiveness and how much more effectiveness is possible.

6. The action taken is continued or discarded.

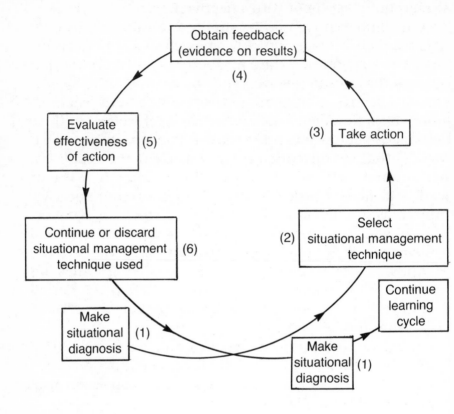

Figure 14.2. Situational sensitivity cycle
Learning, like music, goes around and around

Learning is a continuous process. It is difficult to suggest where it starts or ends. An effective manager is constantly making a diagnosis of the situation, using style flexibility or situational management, and assessing the effectiveness of the action so that an improvement can be made on the nature of the interventions.

So, a manager should not simply respond to situations but should also manage them. A manager should see all situations as opportunities for situational management – that is, opportunities to so arrange the situation that all elements work with, rather than against, each other. Career success is not best explained as a result of luck but as a result of skill used day after day – skill in reading a situation, adapting to it if appropriate, and changing it if necessary and possible. It is hardly necessary to look at formal research studies to make this point. We have all witnessed cases like the one described below.

As with many ambitious young managers, Grimes had ideas about the new job. As the newly appointed marketing manager in a firm that was not marketing-oriented Grimes knew that change would be resisted. By first making a thorough analysis of the situation a plan was then formulated.

The restraining forces that had to be dealt with were carefully considered. A major one was a controller, who made it clear by having an interest solely in budgetary controls and who saw advertising as an expense rather than as an investment. Grimes considered the expectations that the superior, the manager of production, had about the way Grimes would behave in the first few months on the job and to what extent these expectations could be modified. As the situational elements were analyzed, Grimes made a shrewd appraisal of those which had to be adopted and those which could change in the long or the short run. Thought was also given to the president's values and managerial philosophy.

Grimes then worked within the constraints of the system in order to change it – not by a frontal attack on the controller by asking for a doubled budget.

Grimes started by satisfying the controller's desire for tight control, and then by working with the controller on a measuring system for the marketing department's work. This idea was sold to the superior for use in all the superior's departments. Grimes treated each person differently, and waited when waiting was necessary. The firm was seen as an integrated system that had to be studied and understood, not simply as pockets of resistance to the new ideas. Consideration was given as to how to free the marketing function from the production function.

Grimes discovered what advantages the superior, the manager of production, saw in the existing system and what reservations were held about these being moved. Particular consideration was given to the superior's future plans and in what way the marketing department helped or hindered them. Grimes not only considered the total system of which marketing was a part; consideration was also given to each manager individually.

What did Grimes have? We could simply call it good judgement for it was obviously that. A clearer description of Grimes' qualifications would be seen as a manager having self-awareness, situational sensitivity, style flexibility and situational management skills.

Inputs constrain managers, outputs liberate them.

WJR

Experience is a wonderful thing. It enables you to recognize a mistake when you make it again.

Unknown

Chapter 15

Your Profile of Your Scores

Name ....

Month ....

Year ....

INTRODUCTION

This chapter will give you the opportunity to look at your scale scores from all the tests, in one place and at one time. Transfer the scale scores from each of the test chapters to the profile charts following.

For your convenience all the scale definitions and titles are grouped together in Chapter 16 so that in referring to your scores you have easy access to the definition of scales.

While this exercise is useful for you to do alone (to collect things in one place), it will also be useful as a compact format to enable you to discuss your various scores with others.

This chapter of profile charts is *the one part of the book which may be photocopied without permission.* If you plan to meet with a group of managers to discuss your scores and their scores then each would bring this chapter photocopied for each person in the group. A place has been left at the top of this page for your name and the month and year of completion; if they change and their situations change, managers sometimes like to do all or some of these tests again to see what alterations in their behaviour have occurred.

SUMMARY PROFILE CHARTS

Transfer your shadings or hatchings from the relevant test chapters to the summary chart below.

Profile Chart 'A'

	VL		L		ME		H		VH	
	5	15	25	35	45	55	65	75	85	95
Communication Knowledge Inventory (Chapter 3)										
Management Change Inventory (Chapter 4)										
Management Coaching Relations (Chapter 5)										
Management Human Relations (Chapter 7)										
Management Communication Relations (Chapter 8)										
Time Usage Diary (Chapter 10)										

Transfer your shadings or hatchings from the relevant test chapters to the summary chart below.

Profile Chart 'B'
Self-actualization Inventory
(Chapter 6)

	VL	L	ME	H	VH
Physical: Unfulfilled needs concerned with filling biological appetites.					
Security: Unfulfilled needs concerned with maintaining safety and security.					
Relationship: Unfulfilled needs concerned with obtaining love, affection and feeling of belongingness with others.					
Respect: Unfulfilled needs concerned with obtaining self-respect and the esteem of others.					
Independence: Unfulfilled needs concerned with obtaining autonomy.					
Self-actualization: Unfulfilled needs concerned with attaining self-fulfilment.					

Transfer your shadings or hatchings from the relevant test chapter to the summary chart below.

Profile Chart 'C'

XYZ Inventory
(Chapter 9)

		VL	L	ME	H	VH
Factor X	a					
Factor Y	b					
Factor Z	c					

Transfer your shadings or hatchings from the Basic Style Indicator test (Chapter 11) to the summary chart below.

Profile Chart 'D'

Basic Style Indicator Test
(Chapter 11)

	Raw score	0–40	41–80	81–120	121–160	161+
Sep						
Rel						
Ded						
Int						
=	230					

Transfer your shadings or hatchings from the Management Task Inventory (Chapter 12) to the summary chart below.

Profile Chart 'E'
Management Task Inventory
(Chapter 12)

	0–5	6–10	11–15	16–20	21–25	26–30	31–35	36–40	41–45	46+
Executive Z ☐										
Compromiser V ☐										
Ben. autocrat Y ☐										
Autocrat U ☐										
Developer X ☐										
Missionary T ☐										
Bureaucrat W ☐										
Deserter S ☐										

Transfer your shadings or hatchings from the Organization Output Survey (Chapter 13) to the summary chart below.

Profile Chart 'F'
Organization Output Survey
(Chapter 13)

	1	2	3	4	5	6	7	8	9	10
Effective Linking with Subordinates										
Effective Linking with Superior										
Effective Linking with Co-workers										
Authority and Effective Position Design										
Resources to Position										
Climate for Output Orientation										
Benefits of Output Orientation										
Effective Management Information										

Chapter 16

Scale Definitions and Descriptions

INTRODUCTION

This list of scale descriptions is provided for you to have an easy reference to what each scale means for each test. It will be useful when you are looking at your Profile with one or more other people, perhaps discussing the Profile with a colleague or with family members, or in a team of other managers in a training setting.

Authority and Effective Position Design

The degree to which one sees authority in the position as being clearly and appropriately designed.

Autocrat Managerial Style

A manager who is using a high task orientation and low relationships orientation in a situation where such behaviour is inappropriate and who is, therefore, less effective; perceived as having no confidence in others, as unpleasant, and as interested only in the immediate task.

Benefits of Output Orientation

The degree to which output orientation has potential benefits.

Benevolent Autocrat Managerial Style

A manager who is using a high task orientation and a low relationships orientation in a situation where such behaviour is appropriate and who is, therefore, more effective; perceived as knowing what is wanted and how to get it without creating resentment.

Bureaucrat Managerial Style

A manager who is using a low task orientation and low relationships orientation in a situation where such behaviour is appropriate and who is, therefore, more effective; perceived as being primarily interested in rules and procedures for their own sake, as wanting to control the situation by their use, and as conscientious.

Climate for Output Orientation

The degree to which the climate is ready for output orientation.

Communication Knowledge Inventory

A test of general communication knowledge comprising misconceptions of both verbal and non-verbal communication expressing thoughts, feelings and factual data.

Compromiser Managerial Style

A manager who is using a high task orientation and a high relationships orientation in a situation that requires a high orientation to only one or neither and who is, therefore, less effective; perceived as being a poor decision maker, as one who allows various pressures in the situation to have too much influence, and who avoids or minimizes immediate pressures and problems rather than maximizing long-term production.

Dedicated Basic Style

Dedicated behaviour is characterized by high task orientation but low relationships orientation, designated dedicated because of its emphasis on task completion. The dedicated manager tends to be hardworking, aggressive and independent.

Deserter Managerial Style

A manager who is using a low task orientation and a low relationships orientation in a situation where such behaviour is inappropriate and who is, therefore, less effective; perceived as uninvolved and passive or negative.

Effective Linking with Co-workers

The degree to which the relationship with co-workers facilitates the output process.

Effective Linking with Subordinates

The degree to which oneself is using elements of output orientation with subordinates.

Effective Linking with Superior

The degree to which the superior is seen using outputs and effectiveness as a means of managing.

Effective Management Information

The degree to which the management information system is seen as adequate.

Executive Managerial Style

A manager who is using a high task orientation and high relationships orientation in a situation where such behaviour is appropriate and who is, therefore, more effective; perceived as a good motivating force, one who sets high standards, treats everyone somewhat differently and prefers team management.

Integrated Basic Style

Integrated behaviour is characterized by both high task and high relationships orientation and is called integrated because it combines both orientations. The integrated manager prefers shared objectives and teamwork.

Management Change Inventory

A test of knowledge of attitudes towards management principles and practices concerning change.

Management Communication Relations Test

A test of knowledge of sound communication methods; topics covered include communication with subordinates, co-workers, superiors; orders; introduction of change; verbal and non-verbal communication.

Management Human Relations Test

A test of attitude towards others including superiors, co-workers and subordinates.

Managerial Coaching Relations Test

A test of knowledge of sound methods of coaching in these topics: performance appraisal; effectiveness criteria; coaching interview; training.

Missionary Managerial Style

A manager who is using a high relationships orientation and a low task orientation in a situation where such behaviour is inappropriate and who is, therefore, less effective; perceived as primarily being interested in harmony.

Related Basic Style

Related behaviour is characterized by low task orientation and high relationships orientation. It is called related because of its emphasis on relationships with people. The related manager tends to be accepting and friendly and wants to create a secure atmosphere for others to work in.

Resources to Position

The degree to which there are sufficient resources available to perform effectively.

Self-actualization Inventory

Measures the degree to which the following needs are unfulfilled: physical, security, relationship, respect, independence, self-actualization.

Separated Basic Style

Separated behaviour is characterized by both low task and low relationships orientation, i.e. behaviour literally separated from both people and task. The separated manager is really oriented to nothing changing, only to system maintenance.

Theory X Assumptions about the Nature of Man

Man is basically a beast who is best controlled by civilization; who is inherently evil, who is driven by his biological impulses, whose basic interactional mode is competition.

Theory Y Assumptions about the Nature of Man

Man is basically a self-actualizing person who works best with few controls; who is inherently good, who is driven by his humanism, whose basic interactional mode is co-operation.

Theory Z Assumptions about the Nature of Man

Man is basically a rational being open to and controlled by reason; who is inherently neither good nor evil but open to both, who is driven by his intellect, whose basic interactional mode is independence.

Time Usage Diary

An analysis to obtain a clear picture of how time is spent.

XYZ Inventory

Self-information about the underlying managerial assumptions in terms of view of man (and woman) as a beast (X), a self-actualizing being (Y), or a rational being (Z).

Managers should not do things right but do the right things.

WJR

Nobody plans to fail, but many fail to plan.

WJR

Chapter 17

How to Improve Your Managerial Effectiveness

INTRODUCTION

This chapter contains 38 specific recommendations on which you might act. All the recommendations are raised with only one thing in mind – how to help you to achieve an even higher output orientation and therefore managerial effectiveness. As a start, you might like to read over each of the headings to get a general idea of the suggestions made. You may not be able to take action on most of them in the short term, but you can check now some that you think you might want to copy soon. Most of these recommendations arise directly from tests you completed in earlier chapters. One recommendation, such as the one concerning reading, is not discussed elsewhere in the book but will be on your mind.

At the end of the chapter is an action checklist. You may find this a handy method of making decisions concerning these recommendations.

THE RECOMMENDATIONS

The 38 recommendations fall into eight sections:

1. Discussion with others about your test results.
2. Improving your decision making.
3. Giving work away.
4. Recommendations for changes in your behaviour.

5. Reading.
6. Time management.
7. Training and development.
8. Fundamental questions.

Most of the recommendations are directed to the middle or senior manager, and may not relate to your position. If so, you may revise some of them to suit your situation. If you are the CEO or on the top team of a reasonably autonomous unit, there will be many additional things you will want to do to help introduce high output management throughout your organization. Similarly, if you are in personnel or training or are an internal or external consultant, other ideas will come to mind about how you might improve your effectiveness and that of others.

Discussion with others about your test results

There is really no doubt that you should meet with others to discuss your test results; at the same time you may be discussing their test results with them. You need to talk about the test results, to mull over them and to make them part of you. You may decide to change them, and some can be changed. Talk is important.

While, obviously, we are discussing not only test results but also all the things that arise from them, you have a lead here anyway. A good discussion of any test results soon moves off the test and on to you in a more direct fashion. So what is wrong with that? Wait till you try it with your children. They will agree with all the low scores and none of the high scores. Children do this worldwide, I know. So are you person enough to take it? There are some groupings you might want to think about in looking at your trial in the profile charts in Chapter 15 and the definition in Chapter 16. It is best to reproduce each of these on a one-per-person basis for the meetings. The group methods are generally best as they tend to be more objective; where you can, it might be good to get others at the meeting to complete the tests themselves.

Here are some ideas you might want to think about for discussion of your test results. Obviously these discussions start with your test results and extend to your attitudes, your values, effectiveness and so on. However, you have to start somewhere.

1. Discuss with yourself alone
2. Discuss with your superior
3. Discuss with your subordinate team
4. Discuss with your superior's team
5. Discuss with your co-workers alone
6. Discuss with your spouse
7. Discuss with your best friend who knows you and your work
8. Discuss with other friends
9. Discuss with your children
10. Discuss with a psychologist – let us X-ray your nerves!

For all these discussions, plan for a much longer time than you might think necessary. These really are not half-hour, one-hour, even two-hour chats. But set the scene, give them the information in advance, start (whenever possible) early in the morning (say 9am) and don't drink too much before the meeting – preferably not at all!

Discuss with yourself alone
Well, you have it. This is not instant horoscope information – it is real information about how you compare with other managers. A time of reflection, in a place where you can reflect well on your own, might be a good idea.

Discuss with your superior
Why not? What are you scared of? Your superior may be an absolute idiot – it *is* going around these days – in which case you may not want to say anything. Think about whether it might be a good idea. If your superior might use it to 'pounce' then do not undertake the exercise – that is obvious. The best thing then would be

to give your superior the book and see whether there is enough courage to do it with you. This is a two-way situation when both of you have completed everything.

Discuss with your subordinate team
Won't they love it and don't you know it! The way to get even in advance is to arrange that they complete the book as well. Then let's see who is doing what. However, even if you put your scores up, the discussion with them will reveal your willingness to be open and, I know, over time it will rub off. The best thing if all of you are completing the book is to go away for a weekend and plan on a good laugh, a good discussion, and a programme to become effective. It will work. Do not become anxious – we are all different. This book and these tests do not solve everything. If you have a really big problem you might want to bring in some kind of facilitator, but that should only be if both you and one of your subordinates have discussed the facilitator's results as well. Without that, forget it.

Discuss with your superior's team
Do not do this unless they all complete the test results and all agree to go away for a day or two. To do this in a sterile office environment for an hour or so – even for a day or so – will produce nothing. You have to go away for a weekend. It's about telling it as it is, being open, candid, but not overexposing oneself. Again, an outside facilitator might be important.

Discuss with your co-workers alone
Please do not go away with the results with your co-workers alone, as this could immediately turn into a 'bitching' session where you all complain about the people who are not there (which of course includes the superior). These meetings are easy to arrange because everybody likes to moan, but that is not a good way to improve organization effectiveness.

Discuss with your spouse
This can be a good discussion. It depends on your

relationship with your spouse, who does not have to finish the tests although of course it is obviously a good idea. Some of the tests apply to a specific managerial situation and therefore are of less value in evaluating someone who is not in such a position. If your spouse has managerial status then the book must be completed by your spouse before you talk together. If not, pick a few items that seem to apply. If you have some ongoing hidden agendas and hidden quarrels with your spouse that you have not addressed before then these tests will undoubtedly bring them to the forefront in one form or another, but obviously this is not the reason why this book was written.

Discuss with your best friend who knows you and your work

This is just an idea – if there is such a person. As with all these suggestions, consider the other person's needs as well as your own. Your best friend may have wanted to change you for years to be 'more like me'. Sometimes, with a best friend, it is hard to be objective.

Discuss with other friends

My own feeling is that I would avoid this. Friends all like you but often would like to 'have a dig' at you. This is an age-old problem, you may be lucky enough to have some special friends who could discuss your test results with you in a group.

Discuss with your children

'Oh no!', you say – yet out of the mouths of babes and sucklings come wise sayings; like me you will find that children agree with low scales on any test. They will use such comments as: 'I have been telling you this for some time', 'This is why we are the way we are', 'I hope you are person enough to take this comment from an honest, open, clean, sweet, brilliant child of yours', and so on.

Discuss with a psychologist – let us X-ray your nerves!
Do this if you want to. It may or may not help much.
Remember, the psychologist has no idea of what you are
talking about regarding these scales. In all my writings
and work the issue is dealing with the reality, and if you
can deal with reality then in my opinion you do not need a
psychologist. Ask your psychiatrist or psychologist if they
can X-ray your nerves – but only if you think it would help
you!

Improving your decision making

You can learn a great deal from thinking about the
decisions you have made and the ones you should make.
Effectiveness can never be achieved unless the right
decisions are made. Decisions are a manager's stock-in-
trade, and a lack of decision making can lead to pro-
longed low effectiveness. Moreover, in reviewing their
decisions, managers often find that most could have been
made months or years before. Timing is obviously as
important as accuracy. At any one time a manager
usually has several important decisions that should be
made. On some, action is postponed for good reasons; on
others, it is postponed for perhaps no reason at all. There
is no value in making decisions hastily or too far in
advance, but there is often no point in postponing them
for too long either. Managers might well prepare a list of
all the decisions facing them. This is not the usual list of
things to do – it is a decision-list of decisions. This list
should have the most pressing decision (which is not
necessarily the most important) at the top, and can be
used as a guide to action. There is, however, a great
temptation to make the list and then ignore it, or to make
it and then start with the easiest decision rather than the
most pressing one. You are invited to consider these
recommendations:

11. Make a list of your outstanding decisions
12. Make one or more decisions now that you have been
    postponing

13. Analyze your past decisions
14. Make a decision list with timings.

Make a list of your outstanding decisions
A list of your outstanding decisions might surprise you. For some managers it runs to several pages and it is something of a shock. The realization arises that a lower-than-appropriate output occurs not because bad decisions were made but because few were made. Sometimes doing nothing can cause the problem to disappear but that is not the general case. If your list is very long, you will have to start asking yourself some obvious questions.

Make one or more decisions now that you have been postponing
As you make the list suggested above, it will almost certainly become clear to you that some decisions you have been postponing could and should be made immediately.

Analyze your past decisions
It is well worth spending time on analyzing your past decisions. A key question relates to timing. Were some or most decisions made too late or even too early? Do you have a built-in tendency to avoid making decisions which can be revealed by analyzing your past ones? Also consider which decisions were correct in the light of later events and which were clearly incorrect. Analyze the incorrect ones in more detail to attempt to discover what flaws there were in your decision making. For instance, do you characteristically think you have all the facts when, in truth, you do not?

Make a decision list with timings
For as many decisions as possible make a list of when you think each should be made, and do what you can to stick to the list.

Giving work away

One method of becoming an output-oriented manager is to give some of the work away, thus leaving you with more time to concentrate on all those important things you want to do but cannot find time to. The recommendations made here include:

15. Stop doing some things
16. Give some parts of your work away
17. Give your in-basket to your secretary
18. Remove your desk from your office.

Stop doing some things
Make a list of the jobs you do which probably don't need to be done at all. This list is sometimes quite difficult to make on your own and you may need some help with it. Too many managers unconsciously create unnecessary work for themselves and, therefore, for others – they see their job as 'filling in time'. Are there some jobs you could stop doing?

Give some parts of your work away
An effective manager asks about every piece of work that comes up: 'Who below me could handle this?' A manager is not worked out of a job this way – but is worked into the *right* job. A manager may avoid routine administration and spend more time on planning, liaison with other divisions, or the more effective development of subordinates.

Give your in-basket to your secretary
Do you spend too much time rummaging through your in-basket? Are papers brought to you when you want them, or do you let others push their expectations on to you when they want to? Are you somehow seduced into thinking that a full in-basket means you are working at making the right decisions? It is very likely that your secretary has all the capacity necessary to maintain your in-basket for you, let you know what is in it, and make many decisions concerning it. Why not put it to the test?

Remove your desk from your office

This may seem to be a dramatic proposal, and it is. Virtually the only negative result of a trial at removing your desk is your red face when you decide to put it back again! The modern or ancient desk for managers has no real function except to distance visitors to the office and, for the very dim manager, to give an aura of self-importance. Look around your office now and think what could easily be moved out. Yes, most of it. You will be shocked when you come in next morning and find there is no desk and no comfortable in-basket. You will have to start thinking what your job really is rather than thinking that the in-basket should drive you – it will not be there to do it.

Recommendations for changes in your behaviour

19. Make a risk-taking list
20. Experiment with new behaviour
21. Write a letter to yourself about what changes you will make
22. Walk the shop
23. Investigate ways to change your technology.

Make a risk-taking list

A few managers are imprudent and take too many risks. This, however, is the exception – most managers do not take *enough* risks. Some managers with a good level of performance do not take enough risks simply because they want to maintain the existing level of performance with some certainty, rather than attempting to get higher performance through some risk taking. Make a list of risks you could take and think about whether you should make some decisions concerning them. Some advice from someone who knows you and your position would be helpful.

Experiment with new behaviour

Do you hold too many meetings or do you hold too few

meetings? Do you put relationships first or do you put tasks first? Do you spend too much time behind your desk in your office or chatting over tea or coffee? Do you make plans that are too detailed or do you make plans that are not detailed enough? Make a decision to experiment with some particular change in some particular behaviour. Obviously, the best behaviour to start with is that which will not lead to a serious lowering of output if the behaviour change turns out to be incorrect. Another criterion for choosing which behaviour to start with is how soon you can get feedback on the results of your change.

Write a letter to yourself about what changes you will make

Write a letter to yourself and, on the envelope, identify one or two dates on which it should be reviewed and the date when the contents might be evaluated. The letter will concern things that you think you should do. This chapter provides many such ideas and you will have many more of your own. The purpose of writing the letter is to encourage you to think about changes more than you might otherwise, and to give you a chance for self-review. The output-oriented manager is candid about effectiveness in self and others. Based on your understanding of this book, you now have a good idea of what effectiveness is. A good method of improving performance is to obtain or give feedback on performance – that is what being candid about effectiveness leads to.

Walk the shop

Do you get out of your office enough? Do you regularly walk the rounds? Do you make plans to do it very frequently? One CEO of a 35,000-person company spent 40 days one year in having face-to-face meetings with groups composed of every employee in the company. Yes, it was thought to be that important to achieve a higher output. The idea clearly was the correct one. If that CEO could spend so much time, how much time might you spend? Climate is beginning to be seen more and more as an important variable in improving performance in organizations. Walking the shop quite definitely creates a higher output climate.

Investigate ways to change your technology
Briefly, technology is the way work can be done to ensure that effectiveness is the result. Within limits, a manager is able to change technology – that is, able to change the things the manager places emphasis on. This, then, presents one of the most important opportunities to improve effectiveness. Some authority is needed to do this, of course, and it is more likely to be found in managers at the top of the organization or in firms that have a deliberate policy of position flexibility. Effectiveness areas are particularly susceptible to change when the job is new or the manager is new in it, or when a crisis has developed, or when managers operate as a team and are thus willing to engage in flexible job-trading. Some of the many things that a manager can consider when modifying the technology are:

- Emphasizing either task or relationships
- Emphasizing one of planning, directing or administering
- Being either basically an inside or an outside person for the department
- Working with more or fewer subordinates.

Reading

Here are some recommendations concerning reading. Recommendations from authors concerning reading may well be suspect in some quarters, but the simple point is that the author, in particular, knows what goes into a book and how much a book can be helpful if properly used. You are invited to consider these:

24. Re-read this book
25. Get your superior to read this book
26. Get your co-workers to read this book

27. Get all your subordinates to read this book
28. Give a talk on this book
29. Subscribe to, or obtain, on a regular basis, a new management magazine
30. Compile a 'books to read' list
31. Obtain a management article abstracting service.

Re-read this book
The ideas in this book have, literally, greatly magnified the effectiveness of thousands of managers. They can do the same for you but only if you learn them well. Do read this book again.

Get your superior to read this book
Life is much easier when your superior is on your side. You have probably never asked a superior to read a book before. Ask your superior to read this one and to discuss with you what could happen next.

Get your co-workers to read this book
Have you ever recommended a book to a co-worker? Probably not, except in passing. Why not let each of your co-workers know what you think of the book and where they can get a copy. It might convince them if you told them of some behavioural changes that you have made based on reading it. Do not be too concerned if, like most co-workers, they say about the changes you made: 'Well, it's about time – why did you need the book anyway?'

Get all your subordinates to read this book
You can directly influence your subordinates to read this book. If you think the book can help you, then it will help you much more if they all read it.

Give a talk on this book
Giving a talk on outputs is no substitute for reading a book on the subject, though it helps. Giving a talk on this book will greatly help you to integrate the ideas it contains with the good ideas you already have. It would also

help others to begin to think more like you in terms of increasing higher output orientation.

Subscribe to, or obtain, on a regular basis, a new management magazine

Is there a magazine, or possibly several, which you have often thought of reading regularly but have not yet started? It would be a good idea to make a list of these and develop some method of seeing that they come to your attention each time a new issue is published. A good way to do that, of course, is to take out a subscription. With your desk out of the office you will have more time for reading, and reading will help you to improve your output orientation.

Compile a 'books to read' list

You have heard about many books which you have not read. The average book on management takes about eight hours to read. Is there any reason why you could not make a commitment now to read several books over the next twelve months?

Obtain a management article abstracting service

It is a very good idea to subscribe to some form of management article abstracting service. Your business university library may be able to suggest one. In the author's opinion, the best by far is ANBAR Publications Limited, 62 Toller Lane, Bradford BDG 9BY, who abstract articles in the following five areas: Accounting and data processing, Management services and production, Marketing and distribution, Personnel and training, and Top management. The selection of abstracts are published for each of these areas every six weeks. One of the most useful features of the service, for some countries, is that subscribers can obtain the actual article from ANBAR at a moderate cost. The author has been using ANBAR for many years and heartily recommends it for managers who want to be better informed.

Time management

To help you to better manage your time, some recommendations are set out below. Their thrust is to persuade you to analyze how you spend your time. Management starts with a heightened awareness of time, how much time is available and how it is being spent. Some managers have found it useful to undertake a study of their own use of time. They are almost invariably surprised at the results and the lack of effective management displayed. Effective managers need to learn how to create mass undisturbed time and distributed undisturbed time. Mass undisturbed time is particularly useful for projects that involve thinking sequentially, such as writing a report or book. Small blocks of distributed undisturbed time are useful for clearing the desk of the accumulation of notices, memos and travel claims to sign. An obvious short-term way to create mass undisturbed time is by coming in three hours early or doing work at home, but because this may lower effectiveness in the long run, other methods may have to be used. One such method, and there are practical limits in many jobs, is simply to make oneself unavailable on certain days or between certain hours. Most daily interruptions, for many managers, are on relatively trivial matters. As each interruption occurs a manager should ask how it could have been avoided and then modify the decision or information system so that such interruptions either do not occur or at least are minimized. The recommendations are:

32. Start keeping a time record on how you spend your time each day
33. Study how you spent your time for a given past period
34. Plan to structure your time use differently.

Start keeping a time record on how you spend your time each day
Managers who keep a time record almost invariably report how surprised they were at the results. Completing

such a time record need only take a few minutes a day and in some circumstances might be done by the secretary or obtained from an appointment diary. You are asked in this recommendation to spend very little time indeed on studying an important way in which you behave as a manager. It is suggested that you keep your diary for about two weeks.

Study how you spent your time for a given past period
After two weeks or so, make some kind of analysis of how you spent your time. Many bases of such classifications exist and it is best for you to create your own to suit your own situation. You may well want to analyze your time diary in several different ways.

Plan to structure your time use differently
Your analysis will be of little value if you do not make a plan to change the way you spend your time. Make such a plan and develop some method of giving yourself feedback as to how well you are keeping to it and, if not, why not? In making this plan you will find it motivating to think about all the things you have not yet got around to but which you could now do if you get control of your time.

Training and development

Not all managers are in control of time and money needed to take additional training. Some are, and others can often obtain it through good situational management. The world is chock-full of a wide variety of training courses. Some that last a day are useful, as are some lasting several months. Think about those aspects of your job which you could do better if you had just a little more training in them. In a well-designed training course it does not take long for a manager to learn a great deal. There are some excellent training courses that take only three hours – they are rather hard to find but they do exist. As a start, you might want to look around and find out just what is available in your general interest area.

Here are some recommendations concerning your training and development:

35. Make a training and development needs analysis of yourself
36. Investigate what training is available to you from within your company
37. Investigate what training is available to you outside your company
38. Make a training and development plan for yourself covering one to three years.

Make a training and development needs analysis of yourself
What knowledge or skills do you need to make you an output-oriented manager? Start by making a list yourself and ask others who know you and who know about training.

Investigate what training is available to you from within your company
What training can your company provide? Even very small companies have access to a wide variety of training. The astute personnel or training department has a good knowledge, or can obtain details, of courses which are not currently offered from within the company but which could be made available if a sufficient need emerged. Several universities have what they call 'Corporate MBA Programmes' which are the conventional two-year MBA programme done on an in-company part-time basis. If this can be accomplished then most other things can. You may reasonably assume that anything you need to know, or anything in which you need to have a higher skill, can be provided on an in-company basis should the company see a sufficient need and also believe that there would be a reasonable cost benefit for the company.

Investigate what training is available to you outside your company
You may well know, from the number of brochures reaching your desk, that there is a great deal of training

being offered to managers generally, although obviously some courses are better than others. As a starting point, however, it is better to see what is available and then only later try to evaluate one against the other in terms of their suiting your purpose. Obviously, your personnel or training department can be of direct help.

Make a training and development plan for yourself covering one to three years
For how many days a year do you think you could profitably obtain some benefit from training, for which you might reasonably expect to obtain approval? Using this as a base and your knowledge obtained from the two previous recommendations, create a training and development plan for yourself.

Fundamental questions

There are some fundamental issues which managers consider from time to time – you are invited to consider all of them. You are not required to make a 'yes/no' decision on each but are encouraged to think about them. They are:

- A decision that you want to become more effective

- Considering changing your job

- Considering your future

- How you can improve your superior's effectiveness

- How you can improve your subordinates' effectiveness

- How you can improve your co-workers' effectiveness.

A decision that you want to become more effective
It is natural for a manager to say, 'Of course I want to become more effective'. However, in practice every manager is not always prepared to make the effort to do so. Some managers may simply want to mark time until retirement; some may be in the wrong job and any additional involvement would be unpleasant; some are

simply lazy and not inclined to do their best in contributing what they can. Managers must be sure that they really *want* to become more effective before they read about how to do so. So do you want to become more effective?

Considering changing your job

Once they have looked closely at what a job really demands, some managers decide that they are in the wrong job. Sometimes everyone knows it and sometimes no one does. There is a big difference between having daily deadlines and not, between supervising professionals and supervising hourly-paid workers, between system management and selling. It may be that the job is too demanding, not demanding enough, too boring, or involves you in things you would simply rather not do. When one has seen hundreds of managers at work, it takes very little skill to recognize the ones who are in the wrong job. They simply are out of touch. They get no pleasure out of their work. They spend all the time they can doing routine work and avoiding decisions. They are more to be pitied than blamed but they cannot be ignored. Perhaps the salary attracted them and that, together with the pensions scheme, now has them locked in. Perhaps the job demands changed while they were in it. Perhaps, through their own low sensitivity, they did not know what they were getting into – a common example of this is the professional who gets promoted into managing fellow professionals. The ideal solution to being in the wrong job is obvious. The majority of managers who move or are moved from a position in which they are performing poorly, turn out to be more effective and have higher job satisfaction in the new position.

Considering your future

Whether or not the organization has a career plan for you, you should have one of your own. You need to sit down annually and plan where you expect to be in ten years' time. A good start is to list the ages of all your family, your estimated personal wealth, your position, your salary and your accomplishments. Then fill in the ten-year gap with what it is necessary for you to do in order to achieve your plan. The future can simply occur or it can be created. You can see yourself as a cork bobbing on an ocean of fate or as someone with your hand on the tiller in a fresh breeze. The way you see yourself as an effective manager must be understood if you are to create your future.

How you can improve your superior's effectiveness
Most managers would like to be able to influence their superior in some way. There is no better way for a manager to gain such influence than by amply satisfying the superior's expectations. This usually involves the manager directly in becoming effective and at the same time making the superior more effective as well. If your own subordinates could take action to improve your effectiveness then presumably you can do the same for your superior. You are unlikely to do much in the way of changing the style, but you can make the superior more effective. This is particularly possible if the status and power differential between you is low, and if the superior's job is much interwoven with your own and therefore more dependent on you. A superior may also be influenced by using an indirect approach in getting someone else to provide ideas. This influence may be exerted by another manager, a book or article, a consultant or a course. The written word is a much under-used influence, yet it is particularly helpful in the low influence situation which a subordinate is often in.

How you can improve your subordinates' effectiveness
By improving the effectiveness of your subordinates, the effectiveness of the manager is also improved. Perhaps the best single test of a manager is the effectiveness of subordinates. As a minimum this would be expressed by the capacity for one or two of the subordinates to step into the manager's shoes. The most competent way of making subordinates more effective is by giving them challenging responsibilities early in their career. The more challenging the responsibilities, the more effective

the subordinates are likely to become. Effectiveness areas for subordinates are crucial. While the development of managers can be furthered by formal courses, 95 per cent of all real management development goes on in the context of the superior/subordinate relationship. The quality of this relationship determines effectiveness. The superior has by far the most influence in structuring it. A subordinate does not have to model managerial style on the superior in order to become effective, although the younger ones tend to do so especially if the superior appears to be effective, has upward influence and gives them support. Managers usually accept or even welcome such modelling, but the real skill is in recognizing, accepting and managing differences. Managers can be effective in different ways. To force a subordinate into the manager's mould may not work or be necessary. A superior is not running a game called, 'How to be more like me' but instead must demonstrate that subordinates should meet their effectiveness areas, not to please the superior but because their position demands it.

How you can improve your co-workers' effectiveness
Co-workers are usually open to influence at meetings which they attend with you. Managers should therefore think of starting meetings with one of these questions 'What is the objective of this meeting?', 'How will we know if it has been effective?', 'Do we need it?', 'Can we conclude it in 15 minutes?' To do this out of the blue is not always to be recommended but managers should get around to it as soon as they can. Over a period of time it is a relatively simple matter for an effective manager to raise the aspiration level of co-workers by sharing with them the past successes and failures – by describing things as they really are, by suggesting that standards could be much higher and, by personal example, showing that this is what the manager intends to do.

ACTION CHECKLIST

The 38 recommendations listed throughout this chapter are set out below, each followed by Yes, ?, or No. For each recommendation circle one of these three to indicate that you plan to take some action on it in the reasonably near future, or you do not know, or you have decided not to take action. If for any recommendation you feel you are already acting on it, or have done so before and are satisfied that you do not need to do so again, then circle Yes.

Make a list of all of those for which you have circled Yes and put the list into some time frame. The time frame might be immediate, in a few weeks, or some other set of timing that seems satisfactory to you.

YOUR REACTION TO THE RECOMMENDATIONS

A. Discussion with others about your test results

1. Discuss with yourself alone	Yes	?	No
2. Discuss with your superior	Yes	?	No
3. Discuss with your subordinate team	Yes	?	No
4. Discuss with your superior's team	Yes	?	No
5. Discuss with your co-workers alone	Yes	?	No
6. Discuss with your spouse	Yes	?	No
7. Discuss with your best friend who knows you and your work	Yes	?	No
8. Discuss with other friends	Yes	?	No
9. Discuss with your children	Yes	?	No
10. Discuss with a psychologist – let us X-ray your nerves!	Yes	?	No

B. Improving your decision making

11. Make a list of your outstanding decisions	Yes	?	No

12. Make one or more decisions now that you have been postponing	Yes	?	No
13. Analyze your past decisions	Yes	?	No
14. Make a decision list with timings	Yes	?	No

C. Giving work away

15. Stop doing some things	Yes	?	No
16. Give some parts of your work away	Yes	?	No
17. Give your in-basket to your secretary	Yes	?	No
18. Remove your desk from your office	Yes	?	No

D. Recommendations for changes in your behaviour

19. Make a risk-taking list	Yes	?	No
20. Experiment with new behaviour	Yes	?	No
21. Write a letter to yourself about what changes you will make	Yes	?	No
22. Walk the shop	Yes	?	No
23. Investigate ways to change your technology	Yes	?	No

E. Reading

24. Re-read this book	Yes	?	No
25. Get your superior to read this book	Yes	?	No
26. Get your co-workers to read this book	Yes	?	No
27. Get all your subordinates to read this book	Yes	?	No
28. Give a talk on this book	Yes	?	No
29. Subscribe to, or obtain, on a regular basis, a new management magazine	Yes	?	No
30. Compile a 'books to read' list	Yes	?	No
31. Obtain a management article abstracting service	Yes	?	No

F. Time management

32. Start keeping a time record on how you spend your time each day   Yes   ?   No
33. Study how you spent your time for a given past period   Yes   ?   No
34. Plan to structure your time use differently   Yes   ?   No

G. Training and development

35. Make a training and development needs analysis of yourself   Yes   ?   No
36. Investigate what training is available to you from within your company   Yes   ?   No
37. Investigate what training is available to you outside your company   Yes   ?   No
38. Make a training and development plan for yourself covering one to three years   Yes   ?   No

Part IV: Further Application

This last part of the book will be of primary interest to those who want to use it in training settings. First, a variety of hints are given to trainers on how the book might be used in training settings, and then follow some suggestions on how trainers could learn more. Next, the tests available both in this book and elsewhere are listed, and finally a glossary is presented of special terms used.

Chapter 18

Notes to Trainers on Test Administration

PARTS OF THE BOOK YOU MAY PHOTOCOPY WITHOUT ASKING FOR PERMISSION

There are only two parts of this book you may photocopy freely *without asking for permission* – the summary profile charts in Chapter 15 and the scale definitions and descriptions in Chapter 16. The reason that permission is given is that group discussion, using the results from the test and the action plan, is facilitated. If you plan to use group discussion of test results, each participant should be asked to bring a copy for each member of the group. While not its primary objective, making this request does make fairly certain that pre-work is in fact done.

TEST ADMINISTRATION

Here are some ideas on using all or parts of this book in a training setting.

Answer keys

All these tests have built-in answer keys. These were provided to increase the level of involvement and ease of scoring and to decrease the mystique and unnecessary work associated with trainers scoring the tests themselves.

Prior information

Before administering a test always state:

- why the test is being given;
- who will get the results.

Confidentiality

The degree of confidentiality should be specified in advance of test use. It will probably be one of the following:

Only the trainee will know the test results.
Only the trainer will know the test results.
Both the trainee and trainer will know the test results.
Both the trainee and the trainer, as well as the group they are working with at a training seminar, will know the test results.

In training settings, the last-mentioned degree of confidentiality is the best.

Test setting

As most of these tests are used for training it is quite appropriate to say simply, 'Will you fill this out now here [or in your rooms] and then [come back for coffee]'. Many are used as seminar pre-work thereby allowing self-scoring in advance.

Completion in team rooms

Unless deliberately designed for training reasons it is undesirable for tests to be completed in a team or syndicate room. What happens is that test results are shared or discussed, perhaps before the trainer wishes it, and undue pressure is put on the last manager to complete the test hurriedly.

Variable completion time

Some managers take up to 10 to 15 minutes less to complete a test than others. This can cause 'downtime' in well-run courses. It can be avoided by initiating the testing prior to coffee, lunch or end-of-day break, or as pre-work.

Positioning of theory discussion

If a test is to be used simply as a measure of knowledge then a theory lecture on the test subject could precede it. If the test is to be used as a learning vehicle the theory lecture should follow the test or alternatively be postponed until after a group discussion of test answers.

It is inappropriate for the trainer to explain in advance of the test what the test is about, its underlying theory, its scoring scheme or typical scores. All this is best done afterwards, as a prior explanation can bias the response.

Internal validations

Frequent users will wish to validate some tests within their company. This is done by giving the tests to those known to be competent and perhaps also those known to be less competent. The score range of these two groups will serve to validate the power of the tests to discriminate.

Timing

No tests have time limits. If time is short, however, time limits may be imposed, although this should be avoided if possible.

Individual discussion of test results (coaching)

Test results and individual answers may be discussed with the whole seminar at one time, or by each team or

271

syndicate composing it, or directly with the trainee involved.

Such discussion with individuals is not necessary for any test, but can be useful. Helpful questions are:

- Which part of the test do you want to discuss?

- What did you get from the test?

- How widely do you think that answer is viewed as true (or false)?

- How would you come to hold that view?

- Is there anything you want to do as a result of seeing these test results?

Knowledge is not necessarily application of effectiveness

Self-report pencil and paper tests such as these are useful in testing knowledge but are of little value in determining whether the knowledge is being applied. A low score would almost certainly indicate low application, as knowledge is necessary for application. A high score, however, may or may not indicate application as motivation or opportunity may not be present.

Typical programmes of test use

Main room only

	Desirable (hours)	Short (hours)	Long (hours)
Test administered	½	½	½
Team discussion	¾	0	1½
Break	¼	¼	½
Test scored	¼	¼	¼
Scores summarized	¼	¼	¼
Test questions discussed	1	¼	1½
	3	1½	4½

Thus a test could be administered and discussed in a conference setting for 1½–4½ hours.

Main room and team room

	Desirable (hours)	Short (hours)	Long (hours)
Test administered	½	½	½
Team discussion	2	1	2½
Break	¼	¼	½
Team comparisons	½	¼	1
Theory and test discussion	1	¼	1½
	4¼	2¼	5½

Answering questions on test reliability and validity

Reliability is the degree to which a test measures the same thing the same way if re-applied. If a manager took a test twice and got the same score both times, the test would have a high reliability.

Validity is the degree to which a test measures what it says it measures. If a manager obtained a high score on a test purporting to measure communication skill and the manager was a good communicator, the test would have high validity.

Answers to questions raised about reliability and validity may take the form of:

- The face validity (what reading the statements seems to indicate) appears to be high.

- When used as a training tool the test is simply a vehicle for discussion and face validity is satisfactory enough.

- All the tests were constructed by skilled trainers and all tests were inspected by between 10 and more than 100 judges.

- A portion of every test may be questioned and it is appropriate to do so, but the major part of every test is clearly satisfactory for training settings.

Answering questions on specific answers

There will always be disagreement with particular answers, particularly if the majority of the group got them wrong. The trainer should decide which of four positions to take:

- To defend the answer

- To explain the answer

- To take a non-directive position

- To change the answer.

The non-directive position is: 'These tests have been prepared by experts but experts can be wrong. I can see both sides to some of these questions as well. The point for me is whether I accept the overwhelming majority of the answers, and of course I find I can'.

Answering questions on raw score conversions

Some of these tests have a conversion scale which converts raw scores to percentile scores. Participants often object to an apparently high raw score being converted to a low standard score. As an example: 'I got half the questions right, or 50 per cent, yet obtained a score of only 5 percentile'. Explain that percentile does not show an amount of knowledge or attitude but only the relative amount compared to others. A percentile score of 50 shows that the trainee would stand at 50 in 100 managers. A percentage score of 50, however, shows that the trainee has knowledge of half of the test material. If the test is of the true/false variety it could also be pointed out that a child with no knowledge could obtain 50 per cent right by chance alone. Adjustment is obviously necessary.

Chapter 19

How Trainers Can Learn More

INTRODUCTION

You may be very familiar with the use of instruments/ tests/inventories in helping adults – mainly managers in the context of this book – in self-awareness. However, if this is not the case, here are a few ideas to help you on your way.

Some of these ideas are tied in rather tightly to the work of W. J. Reddin and Associates simply because we think we know what we are doing and we have been around for a long time. Other alternatives may well be easily available to you.

The best alternatives would be to consult a management institution, a personnel management institution and, less likely, a management consulting institution or management magazines. The field is still fairly young and fairly small, and thus a call for help to libraries will probably not get you much help at all.

CHOICES AVAILABLE

- Do all these tests
- A discussion of your results with others
- This book completed by others
- Complete all other tests now available
- Start somewhere but do not go mad
- A book you may want to read

- Attend the 3-D managerial effectiveness seminar
- Insights for the output-oriented seminar
- Professional use of instruments seminar
- Other books by Bill Reddin.

Do all these tests

It is obvious that, as a minimum, you must complete all these tests. No one needs defensive reactions such as 'I haven't the time' – we are talking about learning. Also go through the ideas for self-improvement that are suggested to the managers (Chapter 17 – How to Improve your Managerial Effectiveness). If you do not do this you must see yourself as a hero who does not need any personal change.

A discussion of your results with others

Chapter 17 gives some ideas on your discussion of results with others. As you do this you will learn more about the problems encountered with people you are trying to train. It will help you to understand whether things can be done in one hour or one day or intermittently or whatever. It will give you an idea of whether a facilitator is needed sometimes or never. In short, you really have to go through the process or you will not learn.

This book completed by others

If you want to learn more about the tests and what they mean to the individuals who complete them, it would be a good idea to make sure this book is completed by several other people you know fairly well. Then go through a discussion process of some kind – perhaps one-to-one or possibly team-based.

Complete all other tests now available

It can only be a good idea if you get to know other tests available; some are shown in Chapter 20.

Start somewhere but do not go mad

You may need to get more experienced about how people react to test results and how you can best help them – normally by staying out of it and not getting emotionally involved. This has to be learnt by trial and error or under tuition by a coach, and coaches are not always easily available. So, where will you start with your 'hands-on' experience? If all this is rather new to you do not take away your 'Top Team' for a weekend and ask them to complete a management style diagnosis test and then all have a rave-up. This might be your last meeting with them; it depends on your prior experience and skills. You may need to find someone who is not concerned at all by the experience because the experience has been seen many times. Anxiety, as you know, lowers perception enormously and therefore leads to errors. It will take only a couple of experiences to teach you how to handle all this – it is hard to teach it through a book, but make a start somewhere.

A book you may want to read

If you have got this far into this book, *The Output-Oriented Organization* is another you may want to look at. (In no way is this comment part of a book-selling spree; it is merely intended to be helpful.)

The Output Oriented Organization was published in 1988 by Gower (UK) and contains many ideas on how to involve a top team in changing their organization; within about four hours they are all discussing each other's managerial styles happily (yes) and things get off to a good start after that.

The book will give you some ideas. Here is what Reddin and Associates say about it in one of their leaflets:

Top Team Workshops

We specialize in what we refer to as 'Top Team Workshops'. We have been conducting these for more than 20 years. Hundreds of large and small companies have obtained clear improvement in management and organizational effectiveness as a function of them. These workshops are intended exclusively for the Top Team of a single organization. Therefore, the number in attendance normally ranges between five and ten. Those in attendance would be the top person and all immediate subordinates. We normally staff these with two facilitators. The focus of the workshop is agreed in advance and it may be the Top Team. This is a normal and highly effective start: it may focus more on the effectiveness areas and outputs of each team member and the unit as a whole, it may focus on strategy issues or deal with some particular operational problem or problems. The workshop is heavily instrumented . . . by that we mean . . . a very good use of tests for feedback. It seems to run very well.

Attend the 3-D managerial effectiveness seminar

The 3-D managerial effectiveness seminar is planned to take the use of instruments to its limit in helping people to change. It is a six-day residential seminar and has been used for 25 years in 25 countries. You might think about attending if you are interested in the use of instruments for improving things. Here is an extract from the promotional brochure.

This is the 'flagship' seminar of the 3-D Theory of Managerial Effectiveness. Over 100,000 managers have completed this intensive one-week residential seminar. There is extensive mandatory pre-work; teams start at 8.00 am and work until very late at night. The seminar has been used by many well-known organizations such as General Motors, US Civil Service Commission, Westinghouse, Siemens and hundreds of others. One organization had more than 1,700 managers participate. Several other organizations have had over 500 participate. This seminar has been proved to be a highly effective way of improving managerial effectiveness. In addition to the binder, each participant receives textbooks and programme learning books to study in advance of the seminar and a variety of wallcharts to use personally during the seminar itself. The seminar is conducted by staff of W. J. Reddin and Associates or by your own staff. The training to be a staff member consists of participation in one seminar, often the first one conducted on an in-company training, and co-training on three others, again usually in the context of in-company training. This minimum training period is never varied.

Insights for the output-oriented manager seminar

This seminar is devoted entirely to helping managers to come to grips with their scale scores produced by this book. 'To come to grips with' means to relate them to their own effectiveness in your organization and reasons why it might be high or low. Trainers should participate in it and then run it in-company. This is obvious.

Professional use of instruments seminar

A two-day seminar, 'Professional Use of Instruments', is offered regularly in the USA, Canada and the UK and you may be able to have access to it. A brochure is available, and the content of the seminar is set out below.

Topic one: Why use instruments?

Advantages of instruments
Variety of measurements possible
Objective measurement
Flexible uses
Rapid administration and feedback
Comparative data (self or others)
Cheaper than consultant diagnosis
Personal involvement
Provides direction
Leads to action steps

Common client needs for instruments
Objective data
Comparative data
Discussion base data
Open and candid discussion of data
Action plan base data

Characteristics of instruments
Measurement device
Usually self-perception
Usually 'soft' data
Usually psychological or sociological variables
Usually pencil and paper

Main uses of instruments

Administrators use	—	Diagnosis
Objective report to third party	—	Selection/appraisal
Group feedback to strangers	—	Training
Personal feedback	—	Coaching
Group feedback to teams	—	Organization development (OD)

Topic two: Professional use of instruments

Confidentiality
Specify in advance
Play it straight
Options:
    Individual
    Aggregate
    Administrator
    Individual
    Group
    Hierarchy
    'Files'

Things to avoid
    High threat
    Administrator playing 'gotcha'
    Final answer
    Labelling
    Denial – flight
    No chance to work through

Administrator style
    Low threat
    Open-experimental
    Light not heavy
    Confident in instrument
    Using it for client needs

Social desirability effects
    What it is
    When important
    Controls in tests
    Controls in administration

Key statistical terms
    Reliability
    Validity
    Raw scores
    Norms – Deciles – Percentiles
    Correlation
    Item-to-whole
    Standardized test

Topic three: Techniques of use of instruments

Training technique
    Completion of instrument
    Theory input
    Predictions and desirability
    Scoring and posting
    Interpretation of scores
    Discussion
    Action plan

OD technique
    Identification of client
    Identification of client needs
    Discussion of theory and instrument
    Completion of instruments
    Scoring and report
    Pre-work
    Interpretation
    Discussion
    Action plan

Diagnosis technique
    Agreement by client system
    Administration
    Processing
    Analysis by consultant
    Visuals
    Presentation with recommendation

Selection technique
    Target group defined
    Instruments selected
    Two criterion groups obtained
    Administered to both groups
    Cut-off point established
    Validation study

Coaching technique
    Create low threat conditions
    Administer instrument
    Self diagnosis first
        'anything of interest'
        'what agree with'
        'what disagree with'
        'you or situation'
    Defences are functional

Other books by Bill Reddin

Reddin, W. J. *The Smart Manager's Book of Lists*, Lake Publishing Company, USA, 1989, pp 328.

Reddin, W. J. *The Output Oriented Manager*, Gower Publishing Company Limited, 1989, pp 379.

Reddin, W. J. *The Output Oriented Organization*, Gower Publishing Company Limited, 1988, pp 253.

Reddin, W. J. *Managerial Styles Made Effective*, Tata McGraw-Hill, 1988, pp 232.

Reddin, W. J. with Ryan, D. *Handbook of Management by Objectives*, Tata McGraw-Hill, 1988, pp 364.

Reddin, W. J. *How to Make your Management Style More Effective*, McGraw-Hill, 1987, pp 186.

Reddin, W. J. *Effective Management*, Tata McGraw-Hill, 1987, pp 275.

Reddin, W. J. *The Best of Bill Reddin*, Institute of Personnel Management (UK) London, 1985, pp 181. Also published by Harper & Row (Australia), 1985.

Reddin, W. J. *Management Effectiveness & Style – Individual or Situation*, WRA, London, 1983, pp 283.

Reddin, W. J. with Stuart-Kotze, R. *Effective Situational Diagnosis*, Managerial Effectiveness Limited, 1976, pp 192 (Translated in Dutch, Finnish, German, Norwegian, Spanish, Swedish).

Reddin, W. J. *Effectiveness Areas*, Managerial Effectiveness Limited, 1976, pp 185 (Translated in Dutch, Finnish, German, Norwegian, Spanish, Swedish).

Reddin, W. J. with Stuart-Kotze, R. *Money Management*, McGraw-Hill Ryerson, Toronto, 1974, pp 428.

Reddin, W. J. with Kehoe, P. T. *Management by Objectives for Irish Managers*, Mount Salus Press Ltd, Dublin, 1974, pp 234.

Reddin, W. J. *The Money Book*, Scribners, New York, 1972, pp 288.

Reddin, W. J. with Lim, R. *Problems in Business Statistics*, (2nd edition), Tribune, Sackville, 1971, pp 226 (1st edition 1968, pp 78).

Reddin, W. J. *Effective MBO*, McGraw-Hill, New York, 1971, pp 224 (Translated in Danish, Dutch, Portuguese, Swedish).

Reddin, W. J. *Managerial Effectiveness*, McGraw-Hill, New York, 1970, pp 352 (Translated in Dutch, Finnish, German, Portuguese, Spanish, Swedish).

Reddin, W. J. *Campus Countdown*, McGraw-Hill, Toronto, 1967, pp 237.

Reddin, W. J. *Successful Spending, Saving and Investing*, McGraw-Hill, Toronto, 1964, pp 400.

Chapter 20

Tests Available

INTRODUCTION

The eleven tests included in this book have been selected from a much wider range. The purpose of this chapter is to acquaint trainers with other tests available. They may have special applications where these tests would apply. Tests (or instruments or inventories as they are sometimes called) are being more and more widely used in organizations and for adult education generally. Some of the applications include:

- Training
- Management development
- Coaching
- Organization diagnosis
- Organization development
- Self-evaluation and evaluation of subordinates
- Data-based feedback.

Management Style Diagnosis Test

The original test is designed to measure managers and supervisors against the eight styles of the 3-D theory of Leadership Effectiveness. Well over 700,000 managers have completed this test. The test gives scores on many styles such as Deserter, Missionary, Autocrat, Compromiser, Bureaucrat, Developer, Benevolent Autocrat, Executive, Task Orientation, Relationships Orientation and

Effectiveness. Typical items include 'He voices his opinions in public only if he feels that others will agree with him', 'He encourages his workers to make suggestions, but does not often initiate action from them', 'When his superior gives an unpopular order, he thinks it is fair that it should carry the boss's name, and not his own'. Its most common application is in management and supervisory training seminars where its use provokes high interest and lively discussion. It may be fully self-scored by the person completing it. Guides to use are given in the User's Guide.

A brief description of each of the styles as they are, and how they are perceived by others is given in both the test and the manual.

The test measures a manager's perception of his or her managerial style *in the job the manager now has*. For instance, the test does not tell a manager he or she is an 'Autocrat', only that the manager describes his or her own behaviour that way in the job the manager now has. Managers who change their job and answer the test a second time will probably score differently on the test. This will reflect simply that since the job demands have changed, so has the style to deal with them.

Communication Sensitivity Inventory

The Communication Sensitivity Inventory is designed to discover the characteristic response of the manager to others who come to him or her with problems. It presents ten quotes which express problems with superiors, co-workers, subordinates, job, etc. The manager is asked to select one of four responses which best describes what he or she would say. The responses are Feeling, Challenge, More Information, and Recommendation. The test highlights that individual managers typically use only one or two ways to respond to problems. Very useful as a pre-test in courses in listening, coaching and communication. Especially useful if Rogerian 'feeling' responses are being taught.

An example of one of the 'quotes' is given here, together with the four possible responses.

The company policy is supposed to be to hire from within the company. And now I find out that this new guy is coming in to take the place of my boss. I had my eyes on that job; I've been working hard for it. I know I could do the job — I could prove myself if I had a chance. Well, if that's all they think of me, I know when I'm not wanted.

	A			'How do your qualifications compare to that of the new man?' (*This is a challenge response.*)
		B		'Did they discuss it with you at all?' (*This is a more information response.*)
			C	'I would make sure they know your views and let them know your interest in advancement.' (*This is a recommendation response.*)
D				'It's annoying when the company seems to have forgotten about you.' (*This is a feeling response.*)

Sales Style Diagnosis Test

Based on the 3-D Theory of Leadership Effectiveness, this test measures selling style. It is designed as a screening, coaching and training tool for salesmen. The test gives scores on the eight selling styles of Deserter, Missionary, Autocrat, Compromiser, Bureaucrat, Developer, Benevolent Autocrat and Executive, and Task Orientation and Relationships Orientation and Effectiveness. The theory, design and format of the test is based on the Management Style Diagnosis test so far used by over 700,000 managers. This test is widely used because it is highly involving for any salesperson who completes it; it is simple to use and the instructions are printed on the test itself; it is

based on an established salesperson behaviour model; i
stimulates discussion on sales style. The issue of 'Effec
tiveness' is given as much weight as 'Style'; it is an
excellent way to unfreeze and provoke lively discussion.

Management Change Inventory

The Management Change Inventory is an 80 question
true/false test of knowledge of sound methods of introducing change at a worker and supervisory level. Topics
covered include: participation, speed, degree of information, training, resistance, planning. The test is jargon-
free and is usable either before or after training in change
techniques. It emphasizes principles and common sense.
Suggested instructor background reading is Chapter 13
of Reddin, W. J., *Managerial Effectiveness*, McGraw-Hill,
1970, on which most of the test is based. Those scoring
high will be likely to obtain much higher co-operation in
support of proposed changes. Those scoring low will be
likely to focus changes on the system or the paperwork
involved rather than the human beings affected by it.

Educational Administrative Style Diagnosis Test

Based on the 3-D Theory of Leadership Effectiveness, this
test measures the styles of educational administrators. It
is designed as a training tool. It is not designed for use by
teachers except those who are administrative trainees.
The test gives scores on many styles, such as Deserter,
Missionary, Autocrat, Compromiser, Bureaucrat, Developer, Benevolent Autocrat, Task Orientation, Relationships Orientation and Effectiveness. Typical items
include 'He sees students as sources of competent help
and welcomes suggestions from them', 'He believes that
one of the functions of an administrator is that of
keeping accurate records', 'He thinks the involvement of
the educational institution with the community can be

overdone'. Several PhD theses in Educational Administration have been awarded at various North American universities based on research using this test.

Culture Shock Inventory

The Culture Shock Inventory (CSI) is designed to acquaint those who expect to work outside their own culture with some of the things that may get them into trouble. While not yet proven, it appears to have a predictive value. Culture shock is a psychological disorientation caused by misunderstanding, or not understanding, cues from another culture. It arises from such things as lack of knowledge, limited prior experience and personal rigidity. The eight scales test for western ethnocentrism (the belief that the West's way is generally best), cross-cultural experience, cognitive flex, behavioural flex, cultural knowledge specific and general, customs acceptance, interpersonal sensitivity. It may be used with managers, workers, family members and in colleges. The theory behind the test is explained in the manual and can be the basis for a discussion on cultural shock to those going abroad from any country or with those who work with people from other cultures.

Management Coaching Relations

The Management Coaching Relations (MCR) Test is an 80-question true/false test of knowledge of sound methods of coaching subordinates who may be supervisors or managers. Topics covered include: performance appraisal, effectiveness criteria, coaching interview, training. The test is jargon-free and is usable either before or after a discussion of coaching. It emphasizes principles and common sense rather than theory. Those scoring high see coaching as a human relations activity rather than a method of simply teaching skills. These managers believe that a major part of coaching is to enable a subordinate to accept what he or she really knows to be true. Those scoring low tend to see coaching as a manager-based 'tell' session.

Supervisory Potential Test

The Supervisory Potential Test (SPT) is an 80-question true/false test. It is designed to be used solely with potential or new supervisors as a training tool. The test produces eight measures including subordinate evaluation techniques, disciplinary principles, promotion criteria, change introduction, superior relations, new supervisor attachment and subordinate motivation.

Organizational Health Survey

The Organizational Health Survey (OHS) is an 80-question true/false form designed to discover attitudes of managers to the organization, in eight areas. A separate score is obtained for each area which includes productivity, leadership, organization structure, communication, conflict management, participation, human resource management and creativity. This is particularly useful for an organization-wide survey to provide management with information or current opinion, and as an in-company training device using the concensus method. Results may also be used to unfreeze by a discussion of the summary of aggregate responses. The survey is carefully designed so that results may be used for feedback to the top team, self perception diagnosis and unfreezing with those who complete the survey or for top management. It is particularly useful for sequential administrations over the life of an organizational change.

Self-actualization Inventory

The Self-actualization Inventory (SAI) measures the degree to which the following needs are fulfilled: Physical,

Security, Relationships, Respect, Independence, and Self-actualization. Questions are carefully phrased to pulling needs already filled; not 'I enjoy good meals' but rather 'I wish I could enjoy more good meals'. The intensity of the unfulfilled needs is depicted graphically so that a clear need profile is obtained. Statement stems include 'I wish . . .', 'I would like . . .'. A sound use of this test is in association with a discussion of Maslow, Herzburg, McGregor. Useful for comparative studies so managers know how lower levels also answer the test.

Values Inventory

The Values Inventory (VI) is designed to discover a manager's value system. The values tested are theoretical, power, effectiveness, achievement, human, industry and profit. The test consists entirely of quotations from which the manager chooses. Useful for colleges as well as industry.

XYZ Inventory

This (XYZ) Inventory is designed to discover underlying managerial assumptions in terms of views of mankind as a beast (X), a self-actualizing being (Y), or a rational being (Z). Excellent for use prior to discussion of managerial assumptions and especially of McGregor's Theory (X) and Theory (Y). Use of this test could include reading Golding, W., *Lord of the Flies* (Theory X), or seeing the film of the same name; reading McGregor, D. V., *Human Side of Enterprise*, McGraw-Hill, or an associated film.

Communication Knowledge Inventory

The Communication Knowledge Inventory is a test of general communication knowledge for managers. There are 40 questions on communication fallacies, 20 on verbal communication and 20 on non-verbal communication. The non-verbal questions, particularly, make this an unusually powerful and useful instrument.

Supervisory Job Safety

The Supervisory Job Safety test (SJS) is an 80-question true/false test of knowledge of and attitudes toward safety practices. No prior training in safety principles is assumed. Topics covered include: safety instruction, safety devices, safety responsibilities, safety causes, corrective practices, work methods, types of accident, hazard analysis, accident investigation, role of supervisors. The test is jargon-free and is usable either before or after safety training. The test is useful for blue collar supervision but not for white collar supervision. Those scoring high will have a good knowledge of shop floor blue collar 'safety' in the generally accepted industrial sense. Those scoring low will have a poor knowledge of common safety practices in industry. Many white collar supervisors score low as 'safety' is not too important in their situation.

Supervisory Communication Relations

The Supervisory Communication Relations test (SCOM) is an 80-question true/false test of knowledge of sound communication methods. Topics covered include: communication with subordinates, co-workers, superiors, orders, introduction of change, verbal and non-verbal communication. The test is jargon-free and is usable either before or after coaching training. It emphasizes principles and common sense rather than theory. The test is suitable for either blue or white collar supervision. Those scoring high take the view that if the listener does not understand, then the communicator has not communicated. They believe that good communications give equal weight to the needs of the listener and to the needs of the communicator. Those scoring low believe that the best communication is written and formal, and that such things as chairpeople and secretaries of meetings usually aid effective communication.

Supervisory Change Relations

The Supervisory Change Relations test (SCHR) is an 80-question true/false test of knowledge of sound methods of introducing change. Topics covered include: participation, speed, degree of information, training, resistance, planning. The test is jargon-free and is usable either before or after training in change techniques. It emphasizes principles and common sense and a positive attitude towards flexibility. This test is suitable for either blue or white collar supervision. Suggested instructor background reading is Chapter 13 of Reddin, W. J., *Managerial Effectiveness*, McGraw-Hill, 1970, on which the test is based. Those scoring high will be likely to obtain much higher co-operation in support of proposed changes. Those scoring low will be likely to focus changes on the system or the paperwork involved rather than the human beings affected by it.

Supervisory Job Discipline

The Supervisory Job Discipline test (SJD) is an 80-question true/false test of knowledge of accepted disciplinary techniques. No prior training in disciplinary techniques is assumed. Topics covered include: lateness, horseplay, appropriate punishments, corrective interview techniques, handling errors, long coffee breaks, visiting other departments, eating lunch at desk. The test is jargon-free and is usable either before or after training in disciplinary principles. This test is suitable for blue or white collar supervision. Those scoring high believe that discipline is important, and so is the way it is applied. The best way is described as honesty, fairness, firmness and follow-through. Those scoring low tend not to believe in the usefulness of properly applied discipline.

Supervisory Coaching Relations

The Supervisory Coaching Relations (SCORE) test is an 80-question true/false test of knowledge of sound methods of coaching subordinates. Topics covered include: performance appraisal, effectiveness criteria, coaching interview, training. This test is jargon-free and is usable either before or after coaching training. It emphasizes principles and common sense rather than theory. This test is suitable for either white or blue collar supervision. Those scoring high see coaching as a human relations activity rather than a method of simply teaching skills. These supervisors believe that a major part of coaching is to enable a subordinate to accept what he already knows to be true. Those scoring low tend to see coaching as a supervisor-based 'tell' session.

Supervisory Human Relations

The Supervisory Human Relations test (SHR) is an 80 question true/false test of attitudes towards others. Topics covered include relations with superiors, co workers, subordinates. Unlike most of the other OTL supervisory tests a high score on this test indicates only a very positive attitude toward others. It does not necessarily follow that this is the best approach for the super visor in the situation in which he finds himself. A low score, however, does not indicate an essentially negative view. This test is jargon-free and is not a test of know ledge as much as attitude. It is usable either before or after instruction in human relations. It is not recom mended as a test/retest device to discover the effects of training. This test is suitable for either blue or white collar supervision. Those scoring high have a very opti mistic view of workers and their attitudes towards work. They see workers as self-motivated responsibility-seeking individuals who will respond well if treated in a mature way. Those scoring low have a somewhat pessimistic view about workers and work and tend to prefer control, punishment and cash reward as techniques to motivate.

Supervisory Union Relations

The Supervisory Union Relations (SUR) test is an 80-question true/false test of attitudes towards unions. Topics covered include: motives of union leadership, why people join unions, how best to work with unions, management rights, role of shop steward, foreman union relationship, labour benefits, company benefits. The test is well used by asking each supervisor to answer on the basis of what he or she believes is best for the supervisor's position or his company at the present time. Unlike most other OTL supervisory tests, a high score on this test indicates only a very positive attitude toward unions. It does not necessarily follow that this is the best approach for the supervisor in the situation with which he or she must deal. A low score indicates an essentially negative view. The test is jargon-free and is not a test of knowledge as much as attitude. It is usable either before or after discussion of appropriate supervisor-union relations. This test is suitable for either blue or white collar supervision.

Supervisory Job Instruction

The Supervisory Job Instruction test (SJI) is an 80-question true/false test of knowledge of sound job instruction techniques. No prior training in principles of instruction is assumed. Topics covered include: learning principles, teacher-learner relationships, learning aids, learning environment. The test is jargon-free and is usable either before or after job instruction training. The test is suitable for blue and white collar supervision. Those scoring high will be likely to be better at job instruction because they put emphasis on what the worker actually learns to apply rather than what the teacher teaches. They take responsibility for the job knowledge of subordinates. Those scoring low will be likely to think the best teaching is by formal instruction using the lecture technique. They are instructor centred, not learner centred.

Sample Kit

The Sample Kit contains a single copy of 21 tests with supporting instructions and data for each. Those who wish to assess the suitability of any or all of these items are encouraged to first take each test themselves. The Sample Kit is useful to trainers not only as a sample for ready reference, but also to complete for personal development.

TESTS AVAILABILITY

These tests are available from a variety of sources. In some countries exclusive distribution arrangements have been made. Tests are normally supplied only in multiples of ten, with each set of ten also containing a fact sheet on the test and a user's guide. The sample kit may be purchased as a single item.

For your nearest stockist write to:

Kogan Page Limited
Test Division
120 Pentonville Road
London N1 9JN
England

or

Organizational Tests Limited
Box 324
Fredericton
New Brunswick
Canada E3B 4Y9.

I fear explanations explanatory of things explained.
A. Lincoln

If you want to converse with me, define your terms.
Disraeli

Glossary

Basic style: the way in which managers behave as measured by the amount of task orientation and relationships orientation they use. The four basic styles are integrated, dedicated, related, and separated.

Co-worker: a person with whom a manager works who is neither a superior nor a subordinate.

Instrument: as used in training settings, a method of making a measurement or at least taking a reading of some aspect of an individual, a group or an organization. While the terms are technically different the widespread practice now is to use the term 'instrument' interchangeably with 'test' and 'inventory'.

Inventory: as used in training settings, a method of making a measurement or at least taking a reading of some aspect of an individual, a group or an organization. While the terms are technically different the widespread practice now is to use the term 'inventory' interchangeably with 'test' and 'instrument'.

Manager: a person occupying a position in a formal organization who is responsible for the work of at least one other person and who has formal authority over that person.

Managerial effectiveness (E): the extent to which a manager achieves the output requirements of the position.

Norms (norming table): the method of comparing an individual's score on a test with that of others who have completed it, thus allowing the individual to compare self-score with the score of others.

Organization: all the factors which influence behaviour within a social system that are common to essentially unrelated positions.

Relationships orientation (RO): the extent to which a manager has personal job relationships; characterized by listening, trusting, and encouraging.

Self-awareness: degree to which managers can appraise their own style.

Situational management skill (SM): skill in changing the style demands of one or more situational elements so that managerial effectiveness increases.

Situational sensitivity (SS): skill in appraising situational elements in terms of task orientation and relationships orientation demands, flexibility and strength.

Style flexibility (SF): skill in varying one's basic-style behaviour appropriately.

Subordinate: a person over whom a manager has authority and for whose work that manager is responsible.

Superior: a person having authority over another manager and responsibility for that manager's work.

Task orientation (TO): the extent to which managers direct their own and their subordinates' efforts; characterized by initiating, organizing and directing.

Test: as used in training settings, a method of making a measurement or at least taking a reading of some aspect of an individual, a group or an organization. While the terms are technically different the widespread practice now is to use the term 'test' interchangeably with 'inventory' and 'instrument'.

3-D Theory of Managerial Effectiveness: a theory of managerial effectiveness developed by W. J. Reddin. It is known as 3-D because the third dimension of effectiveness is added to the two orientations of task and relationships.

Index